The Crossing

The Crossing

The Curious Story of the First Man to Swim the English Channel

Kathy Watson

HEADLINE

First published in 2000
by HEADLINE BOOK PUBLISHING
10 9 8 7 6 5 4 3 2 1

British Library Cataloguing in Publication Data

Watson, Kathy
    The crossing : the curious story of the first man to swim the English Channel
    1. Swimmers — Biography 2. Long distance swimming — English Channel —
    History
    I. Title
    797.2'1'092

    ISBN   0 7472 2341 6

Designed and typeset by Ben Cracknell Studios
Printed and bound by Clays Ltd St Ives plc

HEADLINE BOOK PUBLISHING
A division of the Hodder Headline Group
338 Euston Road
London NW1 3BH

www.headline.co.uk
www.hodderheadline.com

For my mother

Contents

Acknowledgements   ix

Introduction: Half Man Half Fish   xi

1. A Shropshire Lad   11

2. Hard Biscuits and Hammocks   35

3. The Man is an Obvious Fraud   63

4. A Mere Ditch That Shall Be Leaped   87

5. Too Much Sea   115

6. I'll Stick It as Long as I Can Wag a Toe   129

7. See the Conquering Hero Comes   135

8. What Next?   165

9. Whatever Next!   195

10. A Rum Bit of Water   211

11. Oh, That is Not My Mat   229

Epilogue: A Box of Webb, Please   239

Publishers' Acknowledgements   245

Acknowledgements

I would like to thank the staff at the Ironbridge Museum and the Dover Museum for their help in researching the life of Matthew Webb. A huge debt of gratitude is also due to my agent Patrick Walsh for his help and enthusiasm, and to my husband Paul for his unflagging encouragement and for looking after the baby while I wrote. From among the Channel-swimming fraternity who generously shared their hopes, dreams and insights with me, I would like to single out Alison Streeter, Freda Streeter and Mike Oram. And a special thank you goes to Tim Lawrence who allowed me to accompany him on his own crossing.

A boy's own hero. Webb's swim appears in the comic, *The Hornet*.

Introduction

Half Man Half Fish

He weaker grows! He falters – fails! One half
    mile more for glory!
He lands! that footfall thrills the world! – the
    world shall tell the story

A human link to-day unites fair France and
    England olden;
Webb's name on both grand flags emblaz'd in
    letters pure and golden
Britannia glories in her son! He greater glory
    giveth!
And Matthew Webb's brave name shall live as
    long as England liveth.

        _____ 'Captain Webb' (from The Hornet, 1875)

Shortly after midday on 24 August 1875, a 27-year-old British
merchant seaman called Matthew Webb climbed the steps of the

Admiralty Pier at Dover, paused for a second and then launched himself into the English Channel. Twenty-one hours and 45 minutes later, this 'half man half fish', as a French newspaper promptly dubbed him, walked ashore at Cap Gris Nez in Calais. He was exhausted, delirious and triumphant. Fuelled by a very Victorian diet of coffee, beer, brandy and cod liver oil, he had just swum himself into the history books. He was the first man to swim the English Channel.

I've swum regularly nearly all my life and I first learned of Matthew Webb when I read a 'how to swim better' book called *The Handbook of Swimming*. As well as plenty of training hints, it contained a fairly detailed history of the sport of swimming. Webb had been given a section to himself because, in the writers' opinions: 'A swimming history wouldn't be complete without mention of the legendary Webb.' *The Handbook of Swimming* also reprinted a comic strip story about Webb from *The Hornet*, a boys' magazine. Filled as it was with stories of adventurous men and general derring-do, this comic found Webb the perfect subject matter. 'First to swim the Channel' blazed the headline in large black capitals and added: '"No one can swim the Channel," said the experts, but to Captain Webb the impossible only took a little longer.' I loved the way *The Hornet* made the swim look so easy. The drawings were terrific. The first box shows the Captain, with muscles like a navvy and a huge, handlebar moustache, looking for all the world as if he is coming home in the early dawn from a gay nightclub. He is wearing a striped bathing costume rather like a baby's romper suit and striding into the sea. Behind him, a crowd of ladies and gentlemen, protected from the elements by bonnets and top hats and parasols, watch with interest. Then two experts (a bearded professor and a bowler-hatted doctor) offer their opinions. 'I tell you, Doctor Willoughby, this idea of swimming the Channel is quite absurd,' says Beard. 'The human body cannot stand the strain!' Bowler Hat agrees: 'Quite, professor! The human frame is not constructed for such a feat!'

Next, we have Webb in the sea, as happy as anything, chatting to his friends in the accompanying boat. 'This hot soup is putting new life into me,' he says with a broad grin on his face. He doesn't even look wet, never mind cold. It's not all plain swimming, of course; there are a few setbacks along the way, a jellyfish sting and terrible weather and the gallant Captain does admit to feeling tired. But somehow when he finally walks out of the water at Calais, he may have lost his grin but he looks as rocky and stubborn as when he started. A map of his crossing showed that, although the shortest distance between England and France is 21 miles, the tides meant that Webb had actually swum nearly twice that.

I was 27 when I first read his story – the same age as Webb when he swam the Channel – and I was immediately gripped. At first I was simply overwhelmed by the physicality of his swim. The sheer amount of time he'd spent in the water staggered me. I knew from experience how your shoulders start to ache after just two hours of continuous swimming, how your arms become dead weights and your mind nags at you to stop right now and get out, you've done enough – and he'd been in the water ten times as long. He must have longed to give up, however brave a face he turned to his friends in the boat. The level of hardship voluntarily undergone by Webb impressed and startled me. This wasn't just swimming; this was suffering on a grand scale.

And although since then Webb had slipped into the margins of history, in his day his name had been splashed all over the front pages. His swim made him world famous, swimming's equivalent of Everest's Edmund Hillary. Webb did for the Channel what Roger Bannister did for the four-minute mile. He was regarded with the same sort of awe as this century felt for the first men in space.

These days, most British schools still offer swimming lessons; mastering swimming is one of the milestones of childhood. If participation not observation is the measure, swimming not football or cricket is really this country's national sport. Nearly everyone has been made to do it at some point in their lives and can now do it to a greater or lesser degree. How swimming came to assume this important place in our national and personal culture can be traced back to Matthew Webb.

What I didn't know at the time was that reading that simple little cartoon story would be the beginning of two obsessions – a fascination with Webb and a daydream that one day, perhaps, I too might swim the Channel. From that moment on, if I saw a reference to a Channel swim in the newspapers, I'd cut it out and file it away. I became an armchair expert on the difficulties of long-distance swimming.

Oddly enough, even by the lower standards of his time, Webb was not known as a brilliant swimmer. And by modern standards, his stroke was very slow indeed; I could easily beat him in a race. He swam a good steady breast stroke, but averaged only 20 strokes a minute. These days, it's rare to find a Channel swimmer using breast stroke. It's too slow and the extra time spent in the water increases the chance of hypothermia. But Webb did have the perfect build for open-water swimming. At 5 ft 8½ in and weighing 14 stone, with a 43-inch chest, he was stocky and muscular with the necessary good layer of fat to keep out the cold. (For me, there's something pleasingly subversive about needing to be fat to be good at this sport.) Above all, Webb had the right attitude. The Channel swim is a mental as well as a physical challenge and most swimmers' determination fails before their bodies do. About 50 people attempt it every year; only one in 10 is successful. The swim uses up every atom of the strength you think you have and then demands more. It is not uncommon for swimmers to crawl weeping from the sea, their minds broken, their bodies wrecked. However strong a swimmer you are, every part of your body hurts – your legs, your groin, but particularly your shoulders. Some swimmers have finished using just one arm, the other too painful even to lift out of the water. If you're a man and you neglect to shave really closely, after the many thousands of strokes you will make, the stubble on your chin will lacerate the insides of your arms.

And then there's the cold and the body's weird responses to a prolonged drop in temperature. Even in the heat of summer, the Channel is rarely more than 63 degrees Fahrenheit; that's over 30 degrees below normal body temperature. Some swimmers can't maintain adequate body heat and hypothermia sets in. Their minds begin to wander. They can't answer when spoken to, or alternatively they become hysterical and irresponsible. As the hypothermia becomes more advanced, they start to dissociate or even hallucinate and can no longer make rational decisions about the danger they're in. That's why it's so important that the boat accompanying them is staffed by an experienced pilot and observers. Left to themselves, the swimmer could literally swim into a coma. I read all this and began to wonder what kind of chance I would have of making it.

As my interest in Channel swimming grew, I started checking for Webb's name in the index of any books I read about swimming. Later, I began to research him properly, at first just out of personal interest, then with an evangelistic excitement and a belief that his story was even more intriguing than I'd first imagined.

A Channel crossing remains a formidable achievement. After Webb's feat, it was 36 years and 70 attempts before anyone else succeeded. And Webb held the record for the fastest crossing until 1934, when Edward H. Temme crossed in 15 hours 34 minutes. Since then it's been swum by children and relay teams and people with disabilities; it's been crossed twice and three times. The Captain Webb Plate is awarded to the person who swims the fastest three-way crossing, and is currently held by New Zealander Philip Rush, who swam it in 28 hours and 21 minutes. Webb wouldn't be anywhere near eligible for the honour which bears his name. But first is always first. And Webb swam the Channel when nobody believed it could be done. He backed himself to do it and swam in the face of doubt and even ridicule. Those who followed him knew their goal was achievable.

Not only that, Webb swam it with a number of disadvantages that the modern swimmer doesn't have to worry about. Little was known then about correct nutrition. Alcohol, which the Victorians seem to have considered a medicine, actually lowers the body's temperature and yet Webb drank beer and brandy on his crossing. His swimsuit weighed about 10 lb. By contrast, a modern one-piece weighs just a few ounces, even when soaked. More is known now about navigation and the modern swimmer has the help of detailed weather forecasts and a pilot equipped with radar.

But some things haven't changed. Strip away the technology, the nutritional and training knowledge, and you're still left with the unchanging heart of long-distance swimming – the man or woman who walks down that beach, wades into the water and takes the first stroke. And Matthew Webb's celebrated swim ensured the Channel's starry place in the galaxy of long-distance swims. It's the world's premier swim, the supreme test of a swimmer's courage and endurance. There are longer swims. For example, Lake Michigan — 36½ miles from Chicago to Michigan City. There are colder ones. The temperature of the water in the six-mile strip of sea between Russia and Alaska, known as the Bering Straits, can be as low as 38 degrees and yet it's been crossed. From Cuba to Miami, you're in such danger from sharks you have to swim in a cage attached to your accompanying boat. But in the worldwide community of Channel swimmers, that close-knit, watchful group of people who spend their free time face down in water and who organise their lives according to tides and weather reports, you haven't really made it until you've swum the Channel.

Why this drive to swim long distances? The human attraction to water is so strong that it has been noted by a number of evolutionists. In 1960, distinguished anthropologist Sir Alister Hardy made headlines by asserting a theory that, en route from primitive ape stock to man, there had been a period when food shortages forced us into the water. There, he concluded, we gradually became more aquatic, a sort of wading, diving, fish-catching mammal. Our subcutaneous fat (necessary as a cold insulator) and our hairlessness (making our bodies more streamlined and less resistant in the water) were evidence of this, a sort of ancestral legacy. So too is our love of the seaside and watersports and our adaptability for swimming. 'The fact that some men can swim the English Channel (albeit with training), indeed that they race across it, indicates to my mind that there must have been a long period of natural selection improving man's qualities for such feats,' he maintained.

His speech received lots of publicity, most of it embarrassing; Hardy was dubbed the 'top scientist' who 'claims man is a fish'. Mainstream evolutionists might have preferred to ignore his theory but lofty disinterest became impossible when, from outside their ranks, Elaine Morgan, a TV drama writer (her credits include *Dr Finlay's Casebook*) published *The Descent of Woman, the Classic Study of Evolution* in 1972. In it, she explored and expanded the aquatic ape theory and the book, feminist, witty and highly readable, was an instant bestseller. Desmond Morris in *Man Watching* called the aquatic ape theory 'a brilliant speculation'. It remains fringe and controversial but it has its apologists and keen swimmers like myself rather like it as it seems to give a scientific explanation for our love of water.

I admit that when I first read about Webb I thought he must have been mad. But, after spending a summer interviewing Channel swimmers, I changed my mind. I now think long-distance swimmers are the most well-balanced people I've ever met. It's a sport that brings you face to face with your deepest self; you can't spend that much time alone, in that silent universe, without acquiring self-knowledge. Half-way across the Channel, in the middle of a busy shipping lane, with an aching body and hours of suffering ahead of you, you soon find that any pretensions are stripped away. There is nowhere to hide.

But what do you do when you've done it? For most of us, life is a path bordered with some pleasant flowers and also some brambles, boggy bits where we get stuck and, if we're unlucky, a rock or two where we turn our ankles and have to stop and rest before we can go on. But for people such as Matthew Webb, life is more like a series of mountains to climb. And once you've climbed a mountain, what else is there to do but climb another one? What do you do when you've just achieved the impossible? Well, this is the story of a man who achieved the impossible and what he did next. It is also a story about swimming.

Chapter 1

A Shropshire Lad

You and I must keep from shame
In London streets the Shropshire name;
On banks of Thames they must not say
Severn breeds worse men than they.
_____ A Shropshire Lad, *A. E. Housman, 1896*

His earliest memory was of water. Matthew Webb's childhood was dominated by the long, winding River Severn which ran past his family home in Shropshire. It was his first love and his second home, the place where, as he put it, he first 'became intimate with the element which has since been my great delight'.

The Severn begins life as a thin, brown stream high in the Welsh mountains, streaking out of the slate rocks and peaty bogs near the summit of Mount Plynlimon, in Dyfed and then swelling and meandering north-east through Wales to Shrewsbury. There, it turns south and uncurls through the green fields of Shropshire, Hereford, Worcester and Gloucester before pouring into the Bristol Channel.

Muscular, snaky and, at 220 miles, the longest river in Britain, it writes its name on some of the country's most fertile land and in its journey through thickly wooded Shropshire carves out a deep gorge once seamed with coal and filled with limestone. Legend has it that it was named after Sabrina, the beautiful daughter of Locrine, an early British king who drowned there with her mother, pursued to their deaths by a vengeful and jealous queen. The story appears in Spenser's *Faerie Queene,* Milton's *Comus* and Swinburne's *Locrine.* Loved by poets, overflowing with myth, the Severn was where Matthew Webb, the small boy who grew up to add his name to the history books, learned to swim.

Matthew Webb was born in the small, windswept town of Dawley on 19 January 1848, the Year of Revolution. In Paris, workers, artisans and students had taken to the barricades to protest against the government; Vienna, Prague and Munich were the scenes of demonstrations and riots; and throughout southern Italy, peasants were seizing land and attacking landowners. That year, London was the only major city in Europe not to experience rebellion and Shropshire was a backwater. The turmoil of Europe was a long way from the ordered stability enjoyed by the Webbs. Matthew's father's family had been settled in Shropshire for at least three generations. His great-grandfather, Thomas Webb, had been a medal and button maker but, through his two sons, the family moved out of the artisan class and into the professional, and medicine became the family business. Matthew's grandfather was a popular and successful doctor who, with his well set-up team of greys and the respect of his neighbours, was a perfect model of the typical country physician, a species described by a contemporary wit and observer as 'a well-read and observant man, with a liberal love of science and in every respect a gentleman'. The Webb family always maintained that young Matthew took after his grandfather and a drawing of the old man, comfortably reading his newspaper with his terrier at his feet, shows him to have had the same stocky build, chubby thighs and fair hair of the swimmer. He had two sons, Thomas and Matthew, both of whom followed him into the medical profession.

Matthew, the second son, was even more successful than his father. Parish tithes records note that, by the age of 28, he was a man of considerable property. He owned not only his own house and garden but what amounted to a small estate, including: a second house which he rented out; a croft given over to arable farming; a wooded plantation; a meadow and part of another; three pools; and another house complete with offices, gardens, pleasure grounds, shrubberies, coach road and yards. He married four years later and soon a growing family meant harder work and longer hours. Matthew Webb, the second son, recalled his father leaving the house early every morning, carrying a packet of bread and cheese for his lunch, but there is no reason to believe his assertion that his father's practice was 'more extensive than lucrative'. While far from being one of the old aristocratic Shropshire families or the newer class of wealthy industrialists, the Webbs could none the less count themselves as moderately prosperous. They had all the live-in staff considered necessary by the mid-Victorian middle classes. As well as the family members, the Webb household included a cook, a housemaid, a scullery maid and a governess for the daughters.

Less is known of Matthew's mother, Sarah Cartwright, although her surname hints at old yeoman stock. She was only 23 when she and Dr Webb married in 1845 and her first child, Thomas, was born two years later. The next 17 years of her life were devoted to bearing and raising 14 children. One of them, Alfred, died in infancy. The number of births was not surprising for the mid-Victorian age but the number of children surviving is worthy of note, as infant mortality was frequent at that time. Perhaps their father was a particularly skilled doctor or maybe the Webb children were exceptionally healthy. Certainly Matthew Webb was always proud of his powerful physical strength.

Dawley was a pleasant little town with, as one contemporary visitor put it, 'a most industrious, lively, and upon the whole a very intelligent population'. But the Webbs moved frequently in Matthew's early years, the reason being either an expansion in Dr Webb's practice or their growing family. Matthew was only 14 months old when the family moved to Madeley, a village of about 6,000 people, most of them employed in the iron and china manufacturing works that studded the banks of the Severn. The Victorian travel writer Charles Hulbert described this part of the river as full of boats and business: 'perhaps 150 vessels on the river, actively employed or waiting for cargoes, while hundreds and thousands of busy mortals . . . enveloped in thickest smoke and incessant dust are cheerful and happy'. Other visitors noticed only the dirt and ugliness produced by the factories. One traveller in particular, a Mr Harrall, saw no happy busy mortals and no romance in the River Severn. Instead he was appalled by 'these regions of volcanic-like eruptions, from flaming apertures, projecting huge columns of smoke, intermingled into a dense atmosphere, and groups of sooty labourers like demons of the lower world'. Shropshire was a place of work, hard, back-breaking work and the swelling, busy, unreliable River Severn was a constant reminder that orders had to be filled, goods shipped, money made.

The Webbs were living in Madeley when the River Severn erupted in one of the worst floods the area had experienced for over 50 years. Floods were nothing new in Shropshire. In pagan times, human sacrifices were made to the river gods to appease their wrath and keep the waters from overflowing. In reality, the fury attributed to angry gods was caused by a phenomenon known as the bore, whereby the Atlantic Ocean rushes up the narrow channel at the river's mouth and forces it to overflow its banks. Throughout the Severn's history, eyewitness accounts testified to the speed and terror of its floods. When Matthew was four, the river rose to such a height that, according to the *Shrewsbury Chronicle*, 'that very extraordinary personage, the 'oldest inhabitant', could not recollect Sabrina being so far out of bounds'. The river banks became 'more or less the scenes of destruction and misery'. People grabbed what possessions and livestock they could and headed to the upper storeys of their homes. There they waited with 'in many instances, members of that porcine race, who did not seem much to relish their temporary abode'. Trapped upstairs with bad-tempered pigs, they were aware of the rooms below being flooded; through the windows they saw their furniture being washed out of the house. The streets were like streams, submerged in water several feet deep. The towns looked as if they had been built on a cluster of islands. All sorts of items from beds to bread, chairs to farming implements were seen floating down the river. The brave mounted their horses and swam them across the floods to rescue friends and neighbours. Crops were ruined, property destroyed, and wealthy families became beggars in a matter of hours. Although Matthew never talked about the flood, we can be sure that from an early age he would have been aware of the power and danger of water.

Shortly after the flood, the Webbs moved again, this time settling down for good in a large, handsome, substantially built Georgian house in Coalbrookdale. The gardens were extensive and the River Severn lay, inviting and dangerous, just a field away from the house. Coalbrookdale, which makes an appearance in the Doomsday Book as a small village, had expanded rapidly in the 18th century and now included grand mansions as well as rows of terraces where the factory workers lived. The Quaker Abraham Darby, founder of the Bristol Iron Company, had set his seal on this

The Webb family home in Coalbrookdale, Shropshire.

area, mining its coal, harnessing steam and shaping iron; swiftly it changed from sleepy countryside to the very heart of the Industrial Revolution. The Severn was the area's life blood. Without good communications, all that hard work and technological advancement would have been wasted. Until the coming of the railways, the Severn, bound for the major port of Bristol and easy to navigate, was Shropshire's main link with the outside world. In the year that Matthew was born, it was the second busiest waterway in Europe. Miners, potters, boat-builders and ironworkers toiled along its banks, and it was the highway along which coal, limestone, pottery and iron goods were transported to the rest of the country. And when Darby died in 1717, he left behind a business that would eventually become the largest ironworks in the world. He also bequeathed his own religious tone to Coalbrookdale in the form of an earnest work ethic and high moral standards. Although there were several Quaker meeting houses the Webbs, while never being excessively devout, were Anglicans. Matthew knew his Bible and was particularly stirred by the story of Daniel in the lions' den. Years later, he could describe in detail the roaring lions and the calm Daniel in an old engraving owned by the family. Perhaps he admired Daniel's God-given insouciance in the face of danger.

Less than a mile away was the larger and much busier town of Ironbridge with its weekly market, post office, printing office, drapers, grocery, ironmongers, watchmakers, cabinetmakers, bank, subscription library, ladies' boarding school and boat-builders. Lively and productive, Ironbridge was always full of visitors. Engineers and industrialists came to study the latest developments and journalists to report on any improvements, artists found the industrial landscape a challenge and tourists enjoyed the woods, the glens and the rich green fields, watered by the all-important Severn.

For a healthy, physically robust child who loved animals, bustle and the outdoors, this part of Shropshire would have been ideal. And for Matthew, drawn as he was to the water, having the Severn just a stone's throw from his house was everything he could have wished for. When the weather was warm and the school day over, he and a group of friends would wander down to the river and spend hours there. He always believed that 'The younger the pupil is in

The River Severn where the young Webb learned to swim.

becoming familiar with the water, the easier it will be for him to learn to swim.' He could swim by the age of seven, but he was never able to recall who actually taught him. This suggests he mastered the skill without any of the terrors and aggravations that were inflicted on other boys who tried to learn to swim in the mid-19th century. For this was not a happy time to take to the water. The sport of swimming was growing but it had yet to flourish.

Swimming is as old as the human race and had been a popular pursuit of the Romans, but the centuries succeeding their departure from Britain saw the sport drop away into a rather depressed state. The contempt the Romans felt for the non-swimmer ('he can neither read nor swim' being a particularly withering put-down)

had been replaced by ecclesiastical hostility to any of the manners
or habits of the pagan conquerors. The Church found the nudity of
the Romans' public baths particularly disgusting. Only a few of those
handsome structures with their tiles and mosaics survived. By the
end of the 16th century, official feeling against swimming was so
well entrenched that an extraordinary ruling in 1571 by the vice-
chancellor of Cambridge University caused little surprise. He
strictly forbade students from swimming in the River Cam and set
the most severe penalties for disobedience. An undergraduate caught
swimming would be flogged publicly in their college hall and, on
the following day, in the public schools. A BA would be put in the
stocks and fined 10 shillings.

Yet the lure of water is so strong that there was always resistance. Everard Digby was a Cambridge don but he still wrote an
apologia for swimming, *De Arte Natandi* (The Art of Swimming) in
1587. Swimming, he wrote in defiance of the decree, 'is a greate
help in extreamitie of death and a thing necessarie for every man
to use, even in the pleasantest securest time of his life; especially as
the fittest thing to purge the skin of all external pollutions and
uncleanliness whatsoever.'

Swimming still happened, even with all the disapproval aimed
at it, but it went underground and became a sweet personal secret,
rarely written or talked about. An echo of this can still be seen in
the metaphors that surround swimming. Most sporting metaphors –
'Level playing field', 'play the game' and 'just not cricket' – stress

qualities such as team spirit and fairness. Swimming metaphors, on the other hand – 'plunging the depths', 'keeping your head above water', 'sink or swim' – emphasise individuality and the struggle for survival.

In the end it was the medical profession which rescued swimming from its subversive position and restored it to respectability. In 1754, Dr Richard Russell, a far-sighted physician, began to prescribe sea bathing to his patients. He was clearly very persuasive, or the results were favourable, because he was soon running a large practice at Brighton – in the process transforming a depressing hamlet, inhabited by fishermen struggling to make ends meet, into a lively and fashionable resort – and building himself a handsome mansion on the profits. Not surprisingly, other doctors soon began writing out the same prescription.

Although when Matthew Webb was a child competitive swimming was fairly well developed and a National Swimming Society already in existence, it was still largely confined to the big cities and its popularity restricted to the world of sporting and betting men. It had yet to become a skill taught to every child. For most people, learning to swim was still something you did under doctor's orders. Bathing, as it was more commonly known, was a treatment not a pleasure, to be engaged in for medicinal purposes not enjoyed in its own right. In fact, by the time Matthew Webb was taking his first tentative paddles in the River Severn, cold-water bathing was being hailed as a cure for just about every ailment.

Doctors advised sterile men and infertile women to take it up, and sea breezes were said to restore colour to the wan cheeks of consumptive young ladies, to regulate their menstrual periods and calm their neurotic temperaments. It was believed to heal glandular and venereal diseases, ease the aches of rheumatism, soothe painful corns and bunions, and was even considered effective against some forms of insanity. It was recommended as a way of restoring the ruined constitutions of the dissipated man about town, refreshing the overworked clerk and enlivening the pallid scholar. It supposedly straightened the bent legs of rickety children and reformed the unwholesome thoughts of young people. In fact, the one thing 'a course of bathing' was unlikely to do was create a love of swimming.

For while the sea was seen as hugely beneficial, it was also regarded with terror. It was a restorer of life, but one false move and you could die. Doctor's orders – and there were many – must be obeyed and the result was that for most people swimming was an irritatingly fussy exercise with elaborate rules and petty restrictions. The beach or river had to be just so. A sloping beach facing south, a flowing not an ebbing tide, clear water, no weeds or stones on the bottom. Otherwise you could easily get trapped and drown. There was much debate between doctors about when you should swim – early morning versus midday – but none of them thought you could just plunge in when you felt like it. Swimming outside the summer months was expressly forbidden. You had to pay attention to your diet and eat in moderation but *never* before swimming; the Victorians thought of cramp as so life-threatening that some doctors regarded even a footbath after eating as dangerous.

Your body had to be the correct temperature before entering the water. Too cold and you might develop a chill that turned into consumption or pneumonia; too hot and you were at risk from dying instantly from apoplexy. After the age of 25, you were advised to avoid putting your head underwater; a little judicious wetting of the head was more than enough. There were strict instructions on the length of time to spend in the water (15 minutes was correct, a healthy young boy could occasionally risk half an hour) and how many times a week (two to three times at the most). On no account should you swim to excess as, again, you could easily die, this time from exhaustion. It's no wonder the Victorians though Matthew Webb's 22 hours in the water was a sign of almost superhuman strength. Women were forbidden to swim before or during their periods, while pregnant or breastfeeding, and it wasn't unknown for the poor things to be told to keep their stays on in the water.

Even worse than the rules were the dippers or plungers, sturdy men and women who, for a fee, helped you into the water, first drenching you in sea water; 10 or 12 buckets poured over your head to 'harden you up'. Then – men in the nude, women covered from neck to ankle in a thick flannel gown – it was into the sea where the dippers held your head under the waves a couple of times. Frightened children were forced in, kicking and screaming.

After your dunking, if you still had the inclination, you were left alone for 10 minutes or so to swim on your own. The advice was to imitate the movements of a frog and bathing instructors suggested learners keep tanks of these amphibians in the drawing room and study them. The towel used to dry yourself should be coarse, the clothes put on immediately. Sometimes a stiffish brush was used to produce the 'glow', a heightened state of physical sensation which was bathing's goal.

It was a strange exercise, this mid-Victorian swimming, combining a strict attention to physical safety with a yearning for the intense experience. Doctors all agreed that the best beaches were those with high waves, but the presence of the attendants ensured there was no danger of coming even close to drowning. Secure in the knowledge that you were firmly held and your slightest move watched over by dippers, you could surrender temporarily to the force of the waves dashing against your body and flirt with the pretence of risk. As an experience, it was violent but also cosy, safe but sublime, at one with nature yet highly artificial. It contained few of swimming's real pleasures – that liberating sense of weightlessness, the exhilarating touch of cool water, that transformation from earthbound to water baby, the streamlined movement through another element.

For lucky Matthew Webb, however, swimming in the Severn was just a natural part of a boy's life, an easy extension of play. In his adult life, when he was in demand to give talks on swimming, he spoke out forcefully against common practices like forcing children into the water. 'A child should never be carried out into the deep water and ducked, especially if he shows any fear,' he always stressed. 'Fear of water on his part can never be removed by force or so-called heroic treatment.' And his descriptions of the best way to teach swimming are probably drawn from his own experience and can be summed up simply as: let the child be. 'Let the youngster alone to himself in the shallow water near the shore,' he said.

> He will learn the water like he did walking – a step at a time. Let him go in with others of his own age or older boys and if they go before him he will soon become ambitious to emulate them. This pride will make him do what force or urging never can. He will first learn to swim in shallow water before venturing beyond his depth. Let him swim there as long as he pleases. Do not force him to go into deep water even after he can swim until he feels like doing so himself. His triumph in this respect should be all his own – and it will be a proud one for him.

We can picture Matthew Webb wandering down to some sheltered spot on the Severn, digging his toes into the mud and turning over stones to look at the creepy crawlies underneath. Then paddling in the shallows at first, watching how the other boys swam, copying their arm movements before wading in up to his waist. Perhaps the older boy who taught him walked alongside his small struggling form with a supporting hand under the stomach, patient and watchful until that glorious day, that exquisite, electrifying moment when Matthew suddenly realised he was alone in the water and his teacher was behind not beside him. And his arms and legs were still moving and the water was full and strong beneath his body and his mind whispered with wonder and triumph: 'You're swimming.' We can imagine Matthew Webb, his heart thumping with new confidence, learning stage by stage, minute by minute, to love the water more and more. Every step, every stroke of that journey to intimacy was an adventure. There would be the moment when he realised for the first time that he was out of his depth. A flash of panic and then only delight as he understood it didn't matter, not any more, that the water could support him just as well as the river bottom. From that moment on, there would be no looking back. He would stay in the water longer and longer each time and grumble when it was time to climb out. Emerging from the river would feel like a separation, the water trickling over his back and legs and feet as if it never wanted to let him go. Dry land would feel dull to him, he would miss his body's lightness in water. Then the games would come, fun but testing. 'See if you can swim a width across the river', 'Bet you can't swim two', 'Race you to that tree', 'Who can spend longest underwater' – all this play teaching him to trust the water and himself *in* the water until this new element felt familiar and comfortable. He would find he could turn and twist in the water as easily as a bird changes the direction of its flight in the air and he would do somersaults in the water just for the sheer pleasure of it. Swimming put his mind in touch with his body and unleashed a sense of his own possibilities. Matthew Webb called water 'the native element of man', and considered that a distaste for water could only be attributed to 'natural perversion'.

However many strokes they master, all swimmers have their own stroke, the one that feels just right to them, that allows their body to be most at ease. Matthew's was the breast stroke. 'Good swimming consists in a slow, steady, powerful breast stroke,' he was fond of saying. 'Long, steady, slow strokes make the best swimmer, and in the long run the quickest.' He swam it with his body high on the surface of the water, his head thrown back, arms stretching out high and wide and his legs pushing him forward in the powerful frog-like kick.

He and his older brother Thomas were both strong and confident enough as swimmers to rescue their younger brother Charles when he nearly drowned in the Severn. The little boy had tried to cross the river but found he was too weak to make it to the other side. He'd already sunk beneath the surface by the time his two brothers reached him and dragged him to safety. Matthew was probably only about nine or ten himself at the time.

For the domestic details of Matthew Webb's childhood, we have to thank the fast-thinking John Randall, a Shropshire man who, in the months following Webb's crossing of the Channel, interviewed his friends and family and rushed out *Captain Webb, The Intrepid Champion Channel Swimmer: Original Particulars of his Life*. Randall was passionate about Shropshire: he lived there all his life and extolled its virtues in books such as *The Severn Valley* and *Old Sports and Sportsmen*, a quirky study of Shropshire's forests. He knew Webb's grandfather – his biography is affectionate and charming – and as much about the county as the swimmer. In Randall's loving hands, Shropshire became almost an earthly paradise, a rural English idyll, a land of wood and water and blue, bathed forever in dancing sunlight. He saw it as a place that breeds heroes, men of old England, giants from a golden age. He linked Matthew Webb with other Shropshire lads: the famous and infamous Clive of India and John Benbow, an 18th-century vice-admiral, a good deal less famous but clearly much admired by Randall. He calls him: 'amongst the bravest of the brave . . . One who helped to make England the first naval power in the world.' He was thrilled to note that this landlocked region had produced masters of the ocean. Randall also reminded us of Shropshire's central role in the Industrial Revolution, saluting 'its peaceful champions, its pioneers of improvement', such men of iron as engineer Thomas Telford. And, continued Randall, working himself into a fever of provincial patriotism, 'henceforth it will boast of having given to the world the first man who ever swam the English Channel'. Webb, in fact, spent only 12 years in Shropshire; his time in the Merchant Service was to have a much bigger influence on him.

From Randall we learn that Webb attended the local school along with his brothers. The old schoolfriends interviewed described him as having an 'unbounded fund of fun . . . mirth-provoking drollery and . . . good nature in sharing fruits or sweets'. And he was tough, displaying a combination of fearlessness and exhibitionism in tricks like taking off his shoes, climbing the high iron Buildwas Bridge over the river and walking across the narrow top of the railings, his hands nonchalantly thrust in his pockets. His brother Walter was too frightened even to watch him but Matthew appeared calm and unafraid. In the local dialect so beloved by Randall, young Webb was a 'gallous dog . . . a provincialism signifying venturesomeness'. Another word, less charitable perhaps, would be show-off.

Matthew's parents were cultured in a modest way, filling the house with children's books and encouraging their offspring to read and to paint in watercolours. A favourite family game was giving the children paper and scissors and letting them cut out the shapes of animals. Although he never took lessons, Matthew was keen on drawing, always choosing outdoor scenes and animals rather than people as his subject matter. One of his mother's treasures was a watercolour of a sparrow and a chaffinch, shot by him and then painted and presented to her with the words: 'Here mother, the nobility have their pictures of game, so we will have one of small game.' She doesn't seem to have minded that he kept the dead birds in his bedroom while he was painting them. His family also recalled seeing Matthew's portrait of an exceptionally fat, self-satisfied pig, a duck picking up a grub, a black donkey (nicknamed M. Webb) and the picture he made of a mongoose which had been a present from a family friend who lived in India.

He liked reading, particularly sea stories, and there were plenty to choose from. The 19th-century passion for sailing ships and the men who sailed in them found some of its most vivid expression in children's literature. 'When but 12 years of age, like many youngsters of my own age and of the present day, I conceived a desire for the sea by reading a romance of life on the ocean waves,' Matthew recalled. The romance in question was *Old Jack* by W. H. G. Kingston which he won as a school prize. Kingston was a prolific writer of books for boys and most of his 171 novels dealt with the adventures of young sailors. *Old Jack*, like the rest of Kingston's work, is now largely forgotten but it was so important in firing Matthew Webb's imagination and in determining his choice of career, that it is worth becoming more familiar with it.

The first thing that strikes you is the author's insistence on the truth of the book. Kingston presents himself merely as the conduit, the amanuensis, for the real-life story of a real-life sailor. He introduces us to Old Jack:

> I had more than once, in my rambles in the neighbourhood
> of Blackheath, Greenwich, and Woolwich, met an old man
> walking briskly along, whose appearance struck me as

unusual; but we never even exchanged salutations. One day, however, when I was in company with my friend Captain N. of the Navy, seeing the stranger he stopped and addressed a few words to him, from which I gleaned that he had been a sailor. My friend told me, as we moved on, that he often had conversations on religious subjects with the old man, who had for long been in a South Sea whaler, and had seen many parts of the world. My interest was much excited. I took an early opportunity of making the acquaintance of Old Jack – for such, he told me, was the name by which he was best known; and without reluctance he gave me his history. This I now present to the public with certain emendations, with which I do not think my readers will find fault. W.H.G.K.

There is a point in our childhood when we literally do believe everything we read. And when, as in the case of *Old Jack*, the story's veracity is impressed on us, how could an imaginative boy like Webb fail to be convinced, particularly when the author himself was reduced to initials, as was his friend Captain N., leaving Old Jack as the only fully fleshed character.

Jack was a motherless Irish boy who, after his drunken father was killed in a sectarian fight at Donnybrook Fair, was taken off to sea by some passing sailors. There followed, in the most leaden prose imaginable, a journey to the West Indies with many digressions on the flora and fauna of the islands plus a fair bit of evangelical Christianity and an abolitionist treatise. Old Jack weathered many storms and faced death many times before joining a whaling ship. His mentors were the saintly Peter Poplar and Captain Helfrich who stood in the place of a father to the orphan, teaching him about seamanship and good conduct. There was a sequel to this stirring tale, *Old Jack: A Man of War's Man and South Sea Whaler*, in which Old Jack was taken prisoner on Fiji and faced death a few more times.

Matthew drew heavily on Kingston's portentous style when he later wrote about his own fantasies of a seafaring life. 'Often when I have been lying awake at night, have I pictured to my mind what a storm at sea would be like. Sometimes on windy evenings, when the clouds were chasing each other across the moon, have I crept out of my little bed to the window, and watched the elms tossing their giant arms aloft in the air, and as the wind moaned through them, I fancied that I heard it whistling through the rigging.'

Matthew also liked and owned a copy of Peter Parley's *Tales of the Sea*, one in a series of educational books designed to teach children history and geography. This earnest Boston writer gave his 'little readers' a cheery mixture of facts and then set questions in comprehension at the bottom of each page. Any serious intent was delightfully lightened by his declared belief in sea monsters and krakens. For some reason, though, he drew the line at mermaids.

As with *Old Jack*, the real appeal of *Tales of the Sea* lay not in the didacticism but in the stories of boy sailors whose adventures on the high seas were vividly drawn and highly coloured. Like *Old Jack*, they were pseudo-biographies, fictions masquerading as real-life adventures. Here, Matthew found George Gordon, who ran away to sea and broke his mother's heart, and Leo, the Italian robber who joined a pirate ship and perished when it went down. And James Jenkins, who worked in a whaling ship in the Bering Straits and had his leg bitten off by a shark.

Webb also read and enjoyed the books of Captain Frederick Marryat; his favourite was *Masterman Ready*, a Robinson Crusoe imitation about the Seagrave family who are shipwrecked en route to Australia and become castaways along with Masterman Ready, a pious, elderly seaman. Between them, they make the island inhabitable and fight off savages.

It is clear that Matthew Webb identified himself with these boy heroes and this unsophisticated reading matter fostered two things in him: a longing for an adventurous life and a hope that one day he would be a hero. Popular fiction, the reality of the unknown sea and military triumphalism – it was a naval victory which finally put the terrifying Napoleon in his place – combined to make a seafaring life seem incredibly exciting to Matthew. It held all the thrills that space travel had for the child of the 1960s. Years later, he recalled how:

> Often have I dreamed, or pictured to myself in day-dreams,
> of performing some great feat or act of heroism. I have
> imagined myself commanding a ship, and of being successful

in some great naval engagement. Sometimes I have thought
of performing the feat of rescuing some lovely creature
from some great peril but I must honestly say, that on this
point, considering how young I was, my thoughts were very
vague. It certainly never did occur to me that the great feat
that I should perform and one that would make me a name
in after life would be a feat of swimming.

But there were only a few years in which Matthew was able to enjoy
his child's fantasies. Childhood was short in those days and Matthew
was ready, at an age when nowadays we consider a boy too young for
a paper round, to start working. 'Having so many brothers and sisters,
some older and some younger than myself, I determined, if possible,
to make my own living,' he remembered, 'in what I did not care, so
long as I should not be a burden to them.' So, before he'd even reached
his teens, Matthew Webb's childhood came to an end. What Randall
called 'these days of swimming, boating, birds' nesting, rabbiting, and
fishing, and lying on the river's brim' amounted to at most six or seven
summers. And fond though Webb might have been of Shropshire, he
none the less picked a profession that would take him a long way from
home. The 'faery days . . . bathed in glorious light', slipped into the
past one day in 1860 when, at the age of 12, Matthew Webb, like the
schoolbook hero he was destined to be, went away to sea.

Chapter 2

Hard Biscuits and Hammocks

Here you will put off childhood and be free
Of England's oldest guild: here your right hand
Is the ship's right, for service at command;
Your left may save your carcass from the sea.
Here you will leap to orders instantly
And murmur afterwards, when you disband.
Here you will polish brass and scrub with sand,
And know as little leisure as the bee.

Here you are taught Sea Truth, to eat hard bread,
To suffer with a rigid upper lip,
And live by lookout, latitude and lead.

Here you are linked with Sailors, who abide
The tempest and turning of the tide,
Disaster and the sinking of the ship.

_____ *'The* Conway's *word to the new-comer',*
from Salt Water Ballads, *John Masefield, 1933*

> There is simply nothing to induce a respectable
> man to go to sea – save those few who hope for
> promotion. A sailor's life from the grease-pot to
> the grave, is one continual round of weary labour,
> vexatious tyranny, drunken debauchery and hard
> fare.
>
> _____ *Our Mercantile Marine* by 'an ex-officer', *1872*

Matthew Webb was determined to be a sailor, and after his Channel crossing, he was often described in newspaper reports as having run away to sea, following in the footsteps of his favourite fictional heroes. The truth is more prosaic: once his parents had agreed that Matthew should leave school to go out to work and the Merchant Service (the 19th-century name for the Merchant Navy) settled on as the best place for his particular skills and ambitions, a family friend used his influence to gain Matthew an apprenticeship on the *Conway*, a new training ship recently launched in the Mersey.

He was joining the Merchant Service at a time when its status was at its lowest. It had a reputation abroad for inefficiency and a string of shipwrecks, the loss of life (in one two-year period, nearly 900 sailors died at sea) and the waste of valuable cargo had forced the government to take action. A committee chaired by J. S. Buckingham, the MP for Sheffield, had examined shipbuilders, shipmasters, merchants and nautical surveyors and produced a detailed and damning report. With few exceptions, everything that could be wrong was wrong. Ships were leaky, broken-down and dangerously overloaded with cargo, but overwhelmingly the blame for the tragedies was laid at the door of the men sailing the vessels, in particular the masters. Poorly trained, ignorant of navigation regulations and supplied with inadequate charts, they were a danger to themselves and others. Many lacked basic navigational skills and were miles out in their reckoning of a ship's position. Just about anyone could be given command of a ship. In one instance, the committee found a boy of 14 in charge of a valuable vessel and cargo and in another, a totally inexperienced warehouse porter was entrusted with the position. And they drank. 'Drunkenness, either in the master, officers or men, is a frequent cause of ships being wrecked,' reported the committee. Men slept off drinking bouts at the helm or on the watch and their senior officers slurred contradictory, alarmingly incorrect orders. There were few incentives to improve. Insurance paid out on lost cargo, and restrictions on free trade until 1849 prevented British merchants from using America's far superior trading vessels.

A number of laws were introduced to improve the Service. These included a register of seamen, the establishment of contracts between shipowners and their crews, regulation of their wages, provisions and the amount of space allowed them. Examinations for masters were introduced and the arbitrary, often cruel punishments were outlawed. It was in the spirit of the general uplifting of standards that the Mercantile Marine Service Association of Liverpool and the Western Ports was formed in 1857, its aim 'To take every legitimate step to elevate to their proper position the officers of the Mercantile Marine, and to promote the interests of the service generally . . . to establish schools, afloat and on shore, for the training and education of boys and men for the Service, and generally to do such things as will conduce to the improvement or social elevation of the Merchant Service'. The Association successfully petitioned the Admiralty for a boat to be moored in the Mersey and used as a training school for boys intending to become officers in the Merchant Service. The boat was the *Conway* and, in joining it, Matthew was taking part in a little piece of Merchant Navy history.

The *Conway* was what is known as a 'jackass frigate', that is to say a smallish warship. She weighed 652 tons and could carry 26 guns and 175 men and boys. From her previous function as a coastguard ship, she was transformed into a school and no expense was spared. Her guns were removed and she was thoroughly cleaned, painted and lime-washed. Everything sparkled with newness, a shining testimony to the high hopes and expectations of its ruling committee. The ship was to be run with the same discipline found on the best-regulated vessels, with the aim of turning boys into officers and gentlemen. Smoking, drinking and tattoos were forbidden; in short, the objective was nothing less than the professionalisation, the gentrification even, of the Merchant Service. There was tremendous excitement about the new venture, a sense

Matthew Webb
aged 12.

of being engaged in something fine, and the port of Liverpool was busy and important, its increased trade due to the civil war currently being waged in the United States. Many of the masters resigned excellent positions elsewhere to take up their posts on the *Conway* and there were no problems in recruiting staff; 53 men applied to be the ship's commander. Matthew would have been considered lucky to get a place.

The *Conway* was officially opened in a grand ceremony on 1 August 1859. The first name in the ship's rolls was Berkeley Collins;

he was to become a good friend of Webb and is the source of many of the *Conway* anecdotes about him. Ten months later, on 20 June 1860, in the company of 20 other new boys, Matthew Webb, his head filled with romantic ideas of the sea, his short, plump body dressed in the Conway uniform of blanket trousers, blue jacket with upright collar, gold braid in front of the neck and gilt anchor buttons and cap bearing the badge of the Mercantile Marine Association, came aboard, number 123 on the ship's books. He hated it. 'I was hardly afloat before I wished myself back again to my comfortable home,' is how Matthew remembers that first day and night, 'But it was too late.' He was terribly homesick; from a warm home with close family members, his mother's attention and relative freedom, he was suddenly sleeping in a hard hammock surrounded by strangers and subject to orders. He was physically uncomfortable: there were no sheets on the hammock and the rough blankets rubbed his skin miserably; he was terrified of falling out. 'I am not ashamed to say that my hammock was moistened with burning tears, which, at the time, I would rather have died than allowed the other boys to see,' he recalled.

And yet, by the standards of her time, the *Conway* was a comfortable boat. It was bright and airy, with a large skylight letting in plenty of sun to the upper deck and a wooden grating ensuring that light reached the lower deck too. Thought had been given to the boys' safety and nets were erected to catch anyone who lost their grip and fell from the rigging. A doctor presided over a proper sick room and dispensary. The food allowance was regarded as generous. Matthew had each week: seven pints of milk; seven pounds of bread; 14 ounces of sugar; four ounces of butter (or cheese); one and a half pounds of flour; one pound of rice; one pound of oatmeal; five pounds of fresh meat and one pound of salt meat, both without bone; half a pint of peas; a quarter of a pound of suet; a quarter of a pound of raisins; three and a half pounds of potatoes and vegetables; and tea and coffee as required. As the *Conway* was permanently anchored in the Mersey, the food was fresh.

Matthew soon became reconciled to this combination of boarding school and boot camp. Probably within days, he learned the school slang and started using it. Maybe even by the second night, he would have talked about slinging (sleeping in a hammock), asked his neighbour at table to pass the grease (butter) and talked about covered wagons (fruit tarts) and sodduk (soft bread). Perhaps as a squeaker (a small, noisy cadet), he also tried to niffle (smoke) and was given a clip round the ear by an older boy for being necky (cheeky).

Probably one of the older boys – perhaps Berkeley Collins – took him under his wing and told him about the masters, which ones to fear, which ones to trust. Most important of all was the captain, Richard Mowll – the boys nicknamed him Old Mobby – who was strict but kind, but 'Don't let him catch you with dirty fingernails': he had a horror of them. There was shrivelled-up old Darby with the loud voice. He'd fought against the Turks at the great

sea battle of Navarino and liked to tell war stories. And Moses –
Mosey – Hunt: the joke was that, when he was shouting orders, his
voice carried for an eighth of a mile. His son was on the *Conway* too,
as the gunner. Best of all was the boatswain, Bill Angus; he was a
good old chap but he had no front teeth and made funny noises
when he smoked his pipe.

For two years, Matthew adapted his individuality to this
communal life. He slept in a hammock, just one in a long line in
the dormitory on the lower deck. At six o'clock, he rose, stowed
away his bedding and then queued at the wash place. There were
only four slow-running taps, which made washing a cold, miserable
business in the winter. After that, it was down on his hands and
knees to scrub the deck. Breakfast, taken like all meals in the dining
room, was at eight. Grace was said before and after meals and each
boy kept his own mug, fork and spoon.

After breakfast, the boys were divided into two groups; one
half went to the schoolroom on the upper deck for their general
classes, curtains dividing the large space into separate classrooms.
They sat on long benches and, if Matthew's attention ever
wandered from English and history, mathematics and geography,
he could look at the signal flags, maps and navigational charts
draped on the wall or study the wooden model of the *Conway*
which stood nearby on a table.

Dinner was followed by half an hour's play on the main deck
where the wooden grating on the floor had been reinforced to

withstand the impact of boys running across it. In the afternoon, it was time for the real business of the *Conway*, nautical skills. Matthew learned how to handle the sails, steer a ship, read a map and enough astronomy to navigate. Supper was at five, followed by play and an hour's prep in the schoolroom, then more free time until prayers at half past eight. The boys were in bed by nine o'clock, when the commander and chief officer inspected the ship. There was some variety to the routine at weekends. From Saturday at noon to Sunday evening, boys were allowed to visit friends provided they produced proper notes of invitation.

Boys without invitations could go to the Cornwallis Street Swimming Baths, take a walk in the nearby countryside or spend their money at the tuck shop on Rock Ferry, where a welcome coal fire warmed them in the cold Liverpool winters. Paper chases were popular until local farmers protested angrily about the damage done to crops and they were banned. Wednesday was a half-day, but the boys were not allowed to go far. They stayed on Rock Ferry and tried to play cricket, often giving up because the ground was too rough.

On shore, they were expected to wear gloves and to behave like gentlemen. Loss of leave and stopped pocket money were the most frequently used punishments for transgressors, but the most elaborate methods of correction were reserved for smoking and getting a tattoo. If caught smoking, for example, the offender had a dirty pipe tied with a tarry rope under his nose and was then made to stand on his own so the other boys could see him. Other punishments included standing on deck holding the end of a bench up and, for talking loudly after turning in, the boy was ordered to march up and down on deck for two hours, holding his hammock.

The plan for the *Conway* boys was that they spent two years on the training ship and then went to sea as apprentices. After three or four years, they could sit an examination for second mate. At least another one and a half years had to be passed at sea before they were eligible to take the examination for first mate, and after a further one and a half years of service they were allowed to sit for the much-coveted master's certificate.

It may have been the intention of the *Conway*'s board to take only the better type of boy, but Matthew remembered his companions as a mixed bunch. 'Many of the boys were highly respectable,' he recalled, 'some were highly the opposite.' However he didn't think that 'much that was bad which took place on board the *Conway* was one whit worse than what . . . occurs in many of the highest-class schools in this country'. There was plenty of bullying and Webb, who was small for his age, would have been an easy target. The senior cadets had a Sunday pastime of collecting rubber boots on the lower deck, then ordering the new boys to run away from them and up the ladder while the boots were thrown at them. No doubt the new recruits and the nervous boys were teased with tales of the ghostly sailor on the *Great Eastern* which was anchored nearby. This huge ship, designed by Isambard Kingdom

Brunel, was awaiting repairs but stories abounded of the ghostly riveters who supposedly met their deaths when the vessel was grounded at New York. The noises turned out to be caused by a cable swivel working against a plate but fear of the ghosts drove the bailiffs ashore. When the *Conway* became too small for its intake and the boat was exchanged for a bigger one, the new ship brought its own ghost with it – a marine with his throat cut who disturbed young sailors on the night watch.

Fortunately for him, Matthew Webb was not a nervous boy and he found it easy to make friends. He soon became popular with his schoolmates; his nickname was Chummy Webb. 'Everybody liked him,' a school fellow later recalled. He could hold his own in a fight and firmly believed that 'the boy who will never fight will be sure to get bullied'. There is no evidence that he was more than average at his studies but neither does he seem to have been particularly slow. His instincts, nourished by his early reading, were right – the sea *was* the place for him. Later he credited his time in the Merchant Service with teaching him 'the value of strict discipline – a thing that is good for all to learn'.

The only area in which he stood out was swimming, where he attracted a lot of attention for stamina though not for speed. His smooth, steady breast stroke cultivated on the Severn was easily outstripped and one old boy wrote of him: 'We thought very little of him as a swimmer but admired his staying powers. He could swim about for an hour without putting his foot to the floor, although in a race he was nowhere.' He was fearless in the water. Once when a boy fell overboard, he plunged in without a second's hesitation and hauled him to the lifeboat, winning a silver pencil case as a reward for his bravery.

In 1862, he left the *Conway* with his passing-out diploma and signed a three-year apprenticeship indenture with one William Rathbone, his duty and service now made over to his new master. The Rathbone Brothers were a well-established firm of shipowners, based in Liverpool and operating a fleet of ships which traded mainly in East India and China. From then on, Matthew's visits home would be even rarer. His salary was £30 paid in three parts – £5 for the first year, £10 for the second and £15 for the last. The words of his apprenticeship required him to provide his own clothes and bedlinen, promise to protect the Rathbones' property, keep out of taverns and alehouses and avoid 'Unlawful Games'. In return for this, the Rathbones would teach him the 'business of a Seaman' and provide him with 'Meat, Drink, Lodging, Washing, Medicine and Medical and Surgical Assistance'. Webb signed this indenture on 1 October 1862 and it was duly registered at the port of Liverpool.

At the age of 14, Webb stepped on board the *Cavour* and set sail for Calcutta. It was a difficult trip for a novice, the weather so bad that it took the *Cavour*, a 1,327-ton wooden ship, a fortnight to travel the first 100 miles. In his first week on board, Matthew found himself lurching, terrified, through his first storm at sea. 'For the first time in my life, I experienced what a storm at sea was,' he recalled. 'How far different it was to what I had a few years before pictured to myself, lying in my little bed at home.'

In later years, Webb told many anecdotes about his days at sea but rarely discussed the actual conditions. Fortunately for us, many of his contemporaries lived up to the old sea dog cliché and spun a good yarn, so there are many accounts of life in the Merchant Service. One contemporary of Webb's, J. F. Keane, recorded his vivid impressions of life on a 19th-century wooden boat – and pretty grim reading they make. Keane went away to sea in 1866, after Webb joined the *Conway*; he, too, was only 12 at the time. His *On Blue Waters*, subtitled 'some narratives of sport and adventure in the modern Merchant Service', was published in 1883 and gave a witty account of a sailor's life. He described the food, 'nauseous items', the biscuits, 'that curious adamantine specimen . . . less friable than a grindstone, lacking its brittleness . . . twelve hours soaking in water only rendering it tough and leathery . . . less dangerous to the teeth . . . unhappily indigestible'. These biscuits were famously disgusting, part of sailors' folklore. They were supposed to be made of ground beans but the joke was that the ingredient was actually Portland cement. Keane was obsessed with them, and so too were the ship's vermin. 'The biscuits have a strange attraction for insects and rats . . . swarming with weevils, maggots and consequent dirt and dust.'

Plain duff regularly appeared on ships' menus. This was made of flour mixed with water, then put into a bag and boiled for four or five hours in the copper. 'On Sunday one ounce per man of mouldy currants was added to the flour,' observed Keane gloomily. Split peas were cooked until they turned to mush and were served with salt pork. The beef was black on the outside and tasted overpoweringly of the saltpetre used to preserve it. The tea, coffee and sugar were cheap, nasty and adulterated. A glass of unsweetened lime juice was served daily to keep scurvy at bay. A storm could easily soak and ruin provisions or wash them overboard, so sailors often sailed into harbour in a pitiable state of hunger and dehydration.

Being at sea for so long was boring. Keane recalled reading and re-reading 'cheap works of a most ludicrously immoral or childishly obscene description'. Other forms of entertainment included a 'foo-foo' band, an improvised orchestra made up of the tin kettle, the fog horn, tin plates, forks and sticks. Anything to defuse the tension, irritation, petty quarrels and outbreaks of fighting that inevitably erupted among men cooped up together in a small boat for months on end. There was tragedy too, illness and death, a particularly harrowing experience when the sick man died in the berth next to yours. The corpse was sewn into a sheet and then lowered into the sea while the captain read the burial service.

Although Keane was a wit and a raconteur and no doubt prone to exaggeration, there is no reason to doubt the basic truth of his account. In his travels, he worked with several *Conway* boys and was impressed by their superior qualities. 'A remarkably fine set of boys,' he said. 'They have such an open, manly, English public-schoolboy style about them. The education given them . . . is one of the very fittest that can be conceived as a preparation for the career they propose to follow. Some of them may be a little uppish when they first come on board, but that is a good fault, and keeps them distinct from the men among whom they have to work.' Clearly, the *Conway*'s attempts to improve the class of sailor had worked.

We have no way of knowing how 'uppish' Matthew Webb was, whether he kept himself aloof from the rest of the sailors or whether, when they docked at Calcutta, he followed them to Flag Street, a popular spot with European sailors, being an ill-drained, ill-reputed neighbourhood with grog shops and brothels sited above open sewers. Wild drinking bouts were – still are – part of sailors' relaxation, a sozzled release of pent-up emotion, and, in an 1862 paper, an English doctor based in Calcutta wrote anxiously that half the sickness cases among sailors were due to syphilis. Certainly, Matthew emerged from the Merchant Service in good health, so perhaps he spent his free time on shore admiring the governor's fine mansion and sightseeing in the so-called 'City of Palaces'.

What we do know about Matthew on that first voyage is that, although he was still small for his age, he possessed great stamina and a tough constitution. Despite the hard conditions and the lack of sleep (he claimed to have slept no more than four hours a night), he seemed to thrive on the regime. Seasickness, which frequently felled the new sailors, never bothered him. There was no escaping the usual initiation rites and on one occasion his head was shaved, which he seems to have taken in a good-natured spirit. He also gave himself the traditional sailor's hallmark – a blue anchor tattooed on the right arm.

From the vast port of Calcutta, the ship sailed on to Hong Kong where, having gone ashore, Webb wandered into the wrong part of town and found himself being mugged. He had one dollar in his pocket but was determined to keep hold of it. 'I was horribly frightened,' he recalled. 'But, at the same time, I firmly resolved I would part with my dollar only with my life. I grasped it firmly in my hand outside my waistcoat, and with the other one, I struck my assailants with all my might. I must confess that I kicked also and bit.' When they saw a policeman coming towards them, his attackers gave up the struggle, flung Webb down a steep embankment and made off. Matthew – and his dollar – returned, shaken, to the ship.

From Hong Kong, the *Cavour* sailed to Singapore and from there back to Calcutta and then home. Matthew had been away from England and his family for 17 months, and the consensus at home was that work had made a man of him. He must have seemed very grown-up to the brothers and sisters still at home. But he was soon off again, this time to Aden and Bombay. They stayed in Bombay for three months, where Webb got his first taste of sea swimming. He would swim to one of the other boats in the harbour, eat dinner on board and then swim back. He found he liked swimming in salt water; it was more stimulating than fresh and he enjoyed the extra buoyancy and the rough waves. He liked to observe the sea, noting that the third and ninth waves were often larger than the others, and he respected it. 'You must not attempt to battle with waves,' was always his advice. 'Manoeuvre them and they will assist you.'

Webb must have been a quick learner because, after just his third voyage (Singapore and Hong Kong again), he had sufficient navigational knowledge and expertise to sit and pass his examination for second mate. His indentures expired in 1865, his certificate declaring: 'to the satisfaction of his masters, he is sober and steady, and is a good seaman and navigator'. He chose to leave the Rathbones, however, and went to work as second mate for another Liverpool company, Saunders & Co., sailing their ships to Japan, Brazil and Egypt.

He was the sort of boy that people remember, mainly because of his reckless physical courage and his tendency to flashy exhibitionism. When the deck was crowded with people, he had a habit of climbing the yardarm and then, feet together, arms straight down by his side, he would leap with a shout into the sea. He was still a show-off, at heart still the small boy who stunned his brother by walking along the narrow Buildwas Bridge.

His boldness had its useful side too. Once, in South Africa, he was helping out in the recovery of the cargo from a ship which lay on a shoal about half a mile from shore. In order to retrieve the cargo, a rope was fastened to the wreck at one end and to the shore at the other, making what is known as a surf line along which a boat could be drawn. At night, though, someone had to take the boat out near the wreck, anchor her there and then swim back through the surf. None of the other sailors was prepared to risk it so Matthew earned himself an extra £1 a day for doing it. Matthew was proud of this achievement and often referred to it in later life; in particular he would explain how it taught him to swim in the sea, accustoming his stroke to the push and pull of salt water. 'It is better to dive beneath a long wave than to trust yourself to float over it. Should a huge mass of water be bearing down on you from behind, wait until it nearly reaches you and then suddenly dive downwards, swim a little way under as far as you can against the waves. By this means you will avoid being caught in the crest of the wave. Then turn again and strike out for the shore and let yourself be carried on the huge bend of the wave which will take you rapidly in.' He didn't know it but he was already in training for the Channel.

In the late summer of 1872, Webb read a newspaper account of an attempted swim from England to France and his imagination was immediately fired up. The swimmer was J. B. Johnson, a handsome 23-year-old from Leeds, who had recently taken the London swimming scene by storm with his powerful overhand style of swimming. He was captain of the prestigious Serpentine Club whose members included some of the best swimmers in London, he had a string of medals to his name and was regarded as the 'Champion Swimmer of England'. For some reason, he was always known just by his initials, J.B. He was physically vain and liked to display his strong, muscular upper body and slim hips and was not above deceitful attempts to court attention. A year earlier, he had dived off London Bridge to rescue an elderly gentleman but it later transpired that the man was his brother and a very fine swimmer himself; many people suspected that his announcement that he would swim the Channel was, similarly, a hoax.

Nevertheless, he appeared in Dover on 30 August, dressed to the hilt in a blue coat decorated with white braid and wearing all 40 of his medals. He hired a brass band to accompany him down to the pier and, after three hours of flash and fanfare and watched by an eager crowd, Johnson climbed aboard a steamer, stripped down to his swimming costume and took a header into the sea. After 30 minutes in the water, he seemed to be doing fine. After 45 he asked for a drink of brandy, 15 minutes later, he needed another, bigger one, and 20 minutes after that it was all over. His legs numb with cold, he clambered aboard the steamer, shivering so violently he couldn't even hold the bowl of beef tea that was handed to him. He had lasted just over an hour in the Channel, and the steamer bore him away to France.

News of his attempt had gone ahead of him and, once again, he fancied the credit for something he hadn't done: so just before the steamer glided into Calais harbour, he perked up, dived into the water and swam up to the beach where a large number of people had gathered to greet him. '*Mon dieu!*' they cried. 'Has this man swum from Dover?' 'Yes,' replied the captain of the steamer, 'and he is tired and hungry and wants a bit of lunch.'

Later, Johnson claimed his swim was just a publicity stunt arranged by a Mr Strange, the owner of a music hall in south London where the good-looking J.B. was the star attraction that season. He never, he said, really intended to swim to Calais. It may have been true but it could just as easily have been a face-saving explanation. The following year, he took his embarrassment away with him to America, but for the rest of his career, the 'strange affair' of the Channel, as the newspapers dubbed it, hung over him like a blight.

Strange it may have been but it was at least true and verifiable, unlike the rumour about Salatti, supposedly one of Napoleon's soldiers, who is credited with escaping from a British prison ship and swimming across the Channel to safety. And even if it was only a publicity stunt, it wasn't half as strange or as silly as the case of the English seaman Hoskins who, in 1862, kicked his way across the Channel on a bundle of straw like a real-life Huckleberry Finn. Strange it may have been but it stuck in Webb's mind. It gave him a glimpse into the swimming world which, isolated as he was by constant travelling, he'd known nothing about, and it started him thinking about the Channel. 'The first time the idea of swimming across the Channel entered my head was on reading in one of the papers (I forget which) an account of the attempt Johnson made to swim from Dover to Calais,' he said.

Why, is, of course, the first question that comes to mind. Why would anyone submit themselves to long, dull hours of solitary training and the pain which comes with pushing the body too far, when the odds of success are so slim? Channel swimming cannot be done alone, so although you will find supporters, you must still expose yourself – your hopes, fears and ambitions – to other people. You must turn a deaf ear to their doubts and face down their ridicule. You must spend money – vast sums – on boats and a pilot and crew. And, for all that, however good a swimmer you are, you risk failing like J. B. Johnson did. You can be the champion swimmer of your time but still retire hurt from the Channel. Why? There are dozens of answers, probably as many as there are Channel swimmers.

'I just had to do it,' one successful Channel swimmer explained. 'It was a challenge I could not resist.' The man who holds the record for the greatest number of crossings said: 'Swimming the Channel that first time represented a personal challenge: I wanted to prove to myself that I could do it.' One young man talked in terms of adventure. 'It's the thought that if you don't try something, you never know.' Another recalled his father's fascination with Channel swimming and talked of 'transcendence'. 'It's about yourself,' said one woman. 'The Channel is a living thing and it's about overcoming everything it throws at you. The more challenges you overcome the bigger the adrenalin rush when you walk out the other side.'

Challenge, personal growth, self-testing, proving yourself, showing someone else that you can do it – all these things play a part. What is not there is the wry shrug of the man who, asked why he climbs mountains, replies: 'Because they're there.' You don't swim the Channel because *it*'s there; you swim it because *you* are. Channel swimming is about oneself and crossing the Channel is never less than a rite of passage in the swimmer's life.

Webb became fascinated by long-distance swims. He read about Lord Byron and Lieutenant Ekenhead's swim across the Hellespont in 1810 in imitation of the classical lover, Leander. He seems to have made a detailed study of the story; he knew it well enough to assert that Byron had done the swim in an hour and 10 minutes and Mr Ekenhead in one hour and five minutes, with the tide not in their favour.

His interest in long-distance swimming grew along with his confidence in his stamina. He was looking for a challenge and it came, farcically, in the form of a dog. A Newfoundland dog whose owner, aware of the breed's reputation for courage and swimming ability, boasted that his pet could stay in the water for ages. Matthew immediately said he could do better. Bets were laid and the two competitors – human and canine – tested their stamina in a particularly choppy sea. An hour and a half later, the dog swam back to his master's boat and whimpered to be taken aboard. Matthew was the clear winner and inclined to crow over his exhausted opponent. 'I am disposed to think their wonderful power of endurance has been greatly over-rated,' he said, but was also generous enough to add that 'a chopping sea is not adapted for a dog's style of swimming'. This event was pure Webb. To the end of his life, he loved a challenge, thought little of his own dignity, was fond of a bet and proud of his powers of endurance.

Once, in the Suez Canal, the propeller of his ship got stuck and they were forced to stop. It turned out that the vessel's propeller was being strangled by a thick rope. Someone would have to dive down and cut the propeller free. Webb immediately volunteered and, for the next two hours, he dived under the ship again and again, slashing at the rope until the propeller was released. It was a horrible task, working underwater and in darkness, relying only on your own ability to hold your breath until the job was done.

Finally, it was finished. Back on board, Matthew found an argument in progress. A French vessel had been waiting to pass and the officers on board became impatient. Webb argued back and the French officer gave him a shove. Matthew allowed himself to fall into the water, pulling the officer with him. He was reprimanded half-heartedly and for appearance's sake by his captain, but he and the rest of the crew regarded it as another good joke from Chummy Webb.

This incident may have stuck in his colleagues' memories but his employers never mentioned it, an omission which Webb resented. He liked to excel and he liked it to be noticed that he'd excelled. He left them shortly afterwards and worked his way out to the United States, intending to stay there for a while. However, he took an instant dislike to America and decided to return home. He was to attribute such quick changes to a desire to gain plenty of experience, but it also indicated a restless temperament and a hunger for novelty, two qualities he was to display in greater force later.

He was so keen to leave the States that he agreed to take a position as an ordinary seaman on the *Russia*. This exceptionally fast steamship was the pride of the Cunard shipping line; when she was first launched in 1867, she was said to have the most graceful lines of any ship then sailing, and she could make the crossing from New York to Queenstown in Cork in eight days, five hours and 52 minutes. Passengers loved her; with her leather-upholstered chairs and sofas, her comfortable cabins and her generous five meals a day, she was, in her time, the last word in luxury travel.

On 28 April 1873, the *Russia* was doing her top speed of just over 16 miles an hour under steam and sail. The wind was blowing a gale and some sailors climbed the rigging to take in the sails. Webb was on deck when he heard the cry: 'Man overboard.' A sailor named Michael Hynes had lost his footing and fallen into the sea. Webb ran to the side of the ship and, without even stopping to think, plunged in after him. The waves were as high as houses and the water was bitterly cold, and the ship was moving so quickly that he was soon left behind. Between the heaving crests of the waves, Webb saw Michael's head just bobbing above the surface of the water and thrashed his way towards him, diving through the path churned up by the fast-moving *Russia*. But he was mistaken; it was Michael's cap floating on the surface of the water. The man himself had already

sunk, probably, Webb realised, dragged under the ship and killed
by the blades of the propeller; if the shock of the fall killed him or
if he drowned, that would have been a mercy. But now Webb was
in danger as the *Russia* sailed away.

'I managed to divest myself of my clothing, a thing that was
quite difficult in such a sea,' he recalled.

As I rose, from time to time, to the top of the gigantic
waves I looked anxiously around to see if the ship was in
sight, or any sign of effort to rescue me was apparent but
I could see none, and it began to dawn upon me that I had
been given up and was left alone to a hopeless struggle in
the wild Atlantic. Well, I had this comfort to carry with
me to my watery grave, I had tried to save a fellow man.
Home, friends, the events of my life, all crowded my
brain. I did not quite despair, however, but kept a sharp
lookout.

At last, it seemed an age, I thought I saw a speck on
the crest of a coming wave – was it a boat? I could not
say. It might be fancy only. I thought how hard it was to
die in the prime of health and strength. Again the speck
appeared. It was nearer. It was the boat, but it was being
rowed away from me back to the ship. They had given me
up. In an agony of despair I shouted with almost
superhuman strength, and by God's grace they heard me,

and I was saved. When the boat reached me the sailor in
the boat caught me by the hair, and nearly scalped me in
his endeavour to lift me on board by the natural head
covering.

He had been in the water for 37 minutes. The chances of his saving
Michael Hynes by his action were next to non-existent and he had
arguably put the men in the boat at risk, but praise and rewards
were showered on him. The *Russia*'s passengers clubbed together to
give him a purse of gold. And when he finally reached England, he
learned that he was to be honoured with a gold medal from the
Royal Humane Society of London.

Known as the 'Stanhope Gold Medal', it is awarded to anyone
who has performed a remarkable life-saving act. He was also given
a medal by the Liverpool Humane Society. Both were awarded to
him in May during a grand ceremony at the Freemason's Tavern in
London by the Duke of Edinburgh, one of Victoria's sons. Matthew
was proud of his medals, often wearing them for photographs. 'I
shall always look back upon being the recipient of the first gold
medal given away as one of the most fortunate coincidences in what,
I am bound now to admit, has been a somewhat fortunate career,'
he once said.

Perhaps winning the Stanhope medal gave him the final burst
of confidence he needed because, in the summer of 1874, two years
after reading the J. B. Johnson story, he found his way to the offices

of Robert Watson in Falcon Court, Fleet Street. Watson had been a competitive swimmer; he was now a sports journalist and a publisher. He was to become Webb's lifelong friend and supporter, but he was not impressed when Matthew burst into his office and told him that he wanted to swim the Channel.

Chapter 3

The Man is an Obvious Fraud

The people down on the sand
All turn their head one way
They turn their back on the land
And they look at the sea all day

The land may vary more
But wherever the truth may be
The water comes ashore
And the people look at the sea.

_____ *'Neither Out Far Nor in Deep'*,
from A Further Range, *Robert Frost, 1936*

'I must candidly confess that I doubted a great many of his statements,' was how Robert Watson summed up his first meeting with Webb. The way he saw it, Webb was a perfect stranger who'd simply turned up at his office, asked to see him and then proceeded to regale him with mendacious sailors' yarns. Watson thought of him 'more or less as an interesting trifler with valuable time'. As a swimming enthusiast, he believed in the Stanhope medal – that was there for all to see – but he was inclined to doubt the rest of it, the swimming exploits abroad, the amazing stamina and particularly this Channel idea. But he liked the look of Webb and recalled him affectionately when he wrote his memoirs in 1884: 'He was a fine handsome man with a rollicking, dare-devil, don't care a damn demeanour.'

Webb had read Watson's name in the newspapers and decided he was the man to help him swim the Channel. He chose wisely: Watson was at the heart of the English swimming scene. He acted as referee and starter at dozens of races and was a detailed and meticulous recorder of results. From his Fleet Street office, he published *Swimming Notes and Record,* a six-page weekly magazine aimed at swimmers, trainers, promoters and men who liked betting on races. Every Friday, for the price of 1d, the reader could find out the results of races, details of forthcoming fixtures and browse through adverts for medal makers, swimming lessons and announcements of the opening of new swimming clubs. Watson also wrote a lively, often malicious editorial under the pen name Aquarius. He had an opinion on any question to do with swimming: should the lake in Victoria Park in east London be made available to swimmers (definitely), analysed new swimming strokes as they emerged (he liked the Trudgen, a hybrid stroke with front-crawl arms and breast-stroke legs) and joined in the raging debate about the difference between a professional and an amateur swimmer (nothing wrong with earning money from swimming).

Swimming galas as we know them, with their heats and races of fixed length and qualifying times, were still a long way in the future. Competitions were arranged more or less in the way boxing matches are today – a challenge would be laid down by an individual swimmer, usually in *Swimming Notes and Record* or the sporting paper, *Bell's Life*, and bets invited. There was no fixed length to any of the races and handicaps were often set. The tone of some of these challenges was delightfully peremptory – 'D. Ainsworth, in answer to A. S. Robinson's (of Leeds) challenge, begs to state that he has no time to travel, or he would have met him at Newcastle; but if A. S. is anxious to oppose him, D. A. will make a match to swim him 25 lengths of the Lambeth Baths for a £5 prize' – and frequently acrimonious – 'F. Wilson to W. Struthers. I beg to state in the first place, that his swimming capabilities are of the most meagre character, in proof of which I will take five yards in 120 and run him or give 10 yards in the same distance and swim him.'

Titles were made up: Championship of England, of London, of the Serpentine. Watson knew about all the challenges, all the quarrels and all the friendships. His office doubled as a receiving point for entrance fees to races. He was on nodding, if not always good, terms with all the star swimmers of the day. He knew J. B. Johnson well and thought him 'an extraordinary man', whose swimming was a 'long, beautiful, and machine-like movement'. He also knew and liked Harry Parker, the third best swimmer in England, who taught at the City of London Baths in the Barbican, calling him 'a most unassuming and well-behaved young fellow'. Watson was fond, too, of Harry's young sister, Emily, 'a very clever little girl', who gave demonstrations in floating and diving.

He had no faith in Webb swimming the Channel; he doubted that anyone could do it. Matthew was a stranger to him but Watson had seen Johnson in action, knew his form as it were, and the three-times champion of England had attempted the Channel and failed, failed so totally that he hadn't even managed to stay in the water for an hour. Watson listened to Webb, took him out for a pint at the Mitre in Fleet Street and told him that it was 'better to defer his intended swim until the following year as this season was too far advanced'. Webb agreed, drank his ale, said goodbye and set off for his temporary lodgings in Poplar, east London, promising to return later. Watson promptly forgot all about him.

Watson's advice was just a brush-off but Webb took it seriously. Later that summer, he slipped quietly away to Dover to take his first look at the Channel. He told no one what he was doing, but the solitary sailor with his eyes permanently turned to the sea clearly drew attention. A fellow bather who described himself as 'Captain Webb's Boswell' recalls meeting him on the beach:

I was attracted to him by a certain blunt frankness of manner, and a decidedly gallant bearing. At that time, he

had no employment nor did he appear to have any
determinate object in view. Sailor-like, he appeared to be
merely taking a long rest after a long spell of work, which
he indeed confessed to me was the case. He also expressed
his intention of getting another ship as soon as his stock of
money was exhausted, which he subsequently did.

This new acquaintance was struck by Webb's swimming: 'He
usually went into the water at about 10 a.m., and came out about
12 noon, or 1 p.m., swimming during this time, a distance of two
or three miles out to sea; at others, performing antics in the water,
turning somersaults, standing upon his head &c. More than once
I have lost sight of him altogether for an hour, when he has
returned with an account of having boarded some vessel, and
partaken of a little good cheer.'

The long swims made his face turn red and locals nicknamed
him the Red Indian. They also found him 'modest' and 'temperate
in his habits', and 'altogether an exemplary man for a sailor'. Given
the reputation of sailors, 'exemplary for a sailor' probably means
he only got moderately drunk.

To test himself, Webb swam out to the Varne Buoy, bobbing
in the Channel, about 10 miles off Folkestone. No one witnessed
this so we have to let our imagination do the work. He probably
left his hotel in the quiet morning air, threading his way through
the few early-rising holidaymakers. Down in the harbour, he

undressed, pulled on his swimming suit and found a spot to hide his clothes. Then, quickly, before the cold breeze off the water chilled his resolve, he waded out into the sea and began swimming, his eyes fixed firmly on that spot on the horizon where he knew he would find the Varne Point lighthouse. He would start feeling tired, not bodily tired, but weary in his mind as he contemplated the hours upon hours, minutes upon minutes of cold, arm-aching swimming ahead. Then the rhythm of his strokes soothed him and perhaps the sun came up and warmed his head and he felt the pleasure of it, the joy in having strong arms and legs, and the sweet cool of the water. And, if he was lucky, the pleasure would last, so that when he reached Varne Point, he greeted it not with a gasp of 'half-way there', but cheerfully, before turning round and heading back to shore. Back on land, dressed again in warm clothes, with muscles tingling from cold and exercise, he counted the distance and the time: 13 miles and $4\frac{1}{2}$ hours. Not bad. Not bad at all.

With confidence and determination even higher, he returned to London and presented himself once again at Watson's office. Watson was astonished. 'He respectfully saluted me and said he was determined at all hazards to carry out his object, and had come to seek my assistance,' he wrote in his memoirs. 'I frankly told him that I could not personally busy myself in the matter, in the way he wished, but if he was so anxious, I'd introduce him to one who would possibly be the best medium.' That same day, Watson walked

Webb over the river and down to Lambeth Baths on the Westminster Bridge Road and introduced him to Professor Frederick Beckwith.

Beckwith, Watson could have told Webb, had been 'the greatest swimmer of his day', a one-time champion of England. He now owned a cigar shop in Westminster Bridge Road and ran the swimming club at the nearby Lambeth Baths in Oakley Street where he organised galas, offering the biggest prizes in the business, and trained new swimmers. Competitive swimming had a season – essentially the months of June, July and August – but when winter came, Beckwith by no means shut up shop. Instead, he rented the baths and formed a gymnasium. Week after week, his winter advert could still be found on the front page of *The Swimming Notes and Record*, only now it invited 'swimmers and the public' to come and work out at the 'flying trapeze, stage for boxing, horizontal bars, Indian clubs, rings and, in fact, every gymnastic appliance necessary in an establishment of this description'.

His children – whether by force or by choice – had all followed him into swimming. In 1874, his eldest, William (Willie), was 16 and widely regarded as the most promising swimmer of his age. Watson said that 'besides speed the boy possesses gameness and stamina, two highly necessary and all-important adjuncts'. Both Watson and Beckwith were convinced that, in a year or two, he would beat the great J. B. Johnson. Beckwith's 14-year-old daughter, Agnes, was also a swimmer but instead of racing, she gave displays of 'ornamental' swimming. Dressed in a pink swimsuit with white frills and ribbons, she swam around the pool, first on her front, then on her back, gliding through hoops and floating silent and motionless on the surface of the water while her father explained the principles of swimming to the audience. She was, according to Watson, 'a sturdy, plump little blonde, with large, deep steel-blue eyes, a dumpy nose, full pouting lips, a ready smile, and the least soupçon imaginable of a double chin.' Even the baby of the family, little Charles, played his part; he and Willie would demonstrate the best way to save a drowning man. The family often travelled the country demonstrating their skills and the great professor was not above appearing himself. He would plunge into the pool, waltz in the water and swim with his hands and feet tied together.

Beckwith was short, dapper, wily and a stranger to modesty. In his regular adverts in *The Swimming Record* he called himself: 'This celebrated Ex-Champion Swimming Teacher' and 'the world-renowned swimmer'; his galas were 'world-renowned Swimming Entertainments'. He boasted that he had 'given over 300 prizes towards furthering the interests of this art', and alluded frequently to 'the many celebrated swimmers brought out by him'. Not only did he know about swimming, he knew exactly how to make money out of it and, at first, he didn't like what he saw in Matthew Webb. According to Watson, he 'was not at first impressed with the man or his project'. For a start, Webb swam breast stroke which, while he'd been away from England, had largely fallen out of favour with swimmers, abandoned in favour of side stroke with its faster overarm pull. However, Watson and Beckwith agreed to give this unknown captain a trial. They took a boat out from Westminster Bridge and Webb started swimming.

'The water was very cold, and the surrounding circumstances of sufficient severity to put the swimmer's avowed capabilities to the test,' remembered Watson.

In the most cheerful manner Webb disrobed, and appeared pleased with the opportunity given him of proving the truth of his repeated statements. By the time he was ready to plunge, the bridge was lined with spectators, who eagerly scanned his slow departure, and no doubt wondered what earthly object Professor Beckwith had in engineering such a very slow swimmer. Starting from Westminster with anything but a rapid mode of procession, he reached Waterloo Bridge in 10 minutes, and sped on to the Blackfriars structure, which occupied 20 minutes 10 seconds. Before passing under Southwark Bridge he received the assistance tide, the time at the last-named edifice being 28 minutes 15 seconds. In 32 minutes 40 seconds he went through London Bridge and passed the Tower in 40 minutes 40 seconds.

On the boat Beckwith and Watson were becoming restless. 'He swam until we were tired of looking at him,' remembered Watson.

Webb wears with pride his two Stanhope medals for bravery.

'He proposed to go seaward, turn with the tide and swim back. This amazed Beckwith, who remarked: "If you do, you'll not have me for a companion. I'm off." Whereupon Webb was hauled into the boat. We were satisfied that he was then a very marvellous man.'

Webb had won his first battle – he'd convinced these two important men that it was worth launching him, he'd gained their respect and he'd made new friends. Although he didn't know it, he was lucky in that he'd met Beckwith at the point when the professor was looking for a new swimmer to add to his team. He'd been engaged in a long-running competition with Harry Parker and, although his son Willie's swimming was a credit to Beckwith, he liked to have another card to play.

Throughout the autumn of 1874, Webb trained at the Lambeth Baths. They were the largest municipal baths in London, built in the first wave of enthusiasm after the 1848 Baths and Wash-houses Act gave local authorities the power to build baths and pools to relieve some of the terrible diseases and problems caused by urban overcrowding and poor hygiene. For their time, they were a model of what swimming baths should be, being clean, well ventilated and well lit, the high sloping ceiling filled with windows letting in daylight. There were two baths, one 41 yards by 15, the other 38 yards by 18. Webb used to arrive early every morning, undress in one of the eight boxes on the side of the baths, push open the half-door and walk across the paved path to the water. It was his first taste of indoor swimming; he was used to muddy river and sandy sea bottom below him, not coloured tiles. And the sense of confinement, his space marked out by white porcelain rather than the green banks of the river or the sandy shore or anchored ship was a novelty. He spent whole days at the baths, perching on the diving board for a rest between sessions. Hour after hour he swam slowly round the baths, enjoying the solitude and waiting until the gas was lit before climbing out of the pool, drinking a glass of ale and returning home to Poplar. He was always alone, and after a couple of weeks the bath superintendent became suspicious, confiding to Watson that he was sure the man was there for some reason other than swimming. Watson had to reassure him that Webb was a friend of both himself and Beckwith.

Matthew was still in training when another strange affair happened and another claimant to the Channel appeared. He was an even bigger publicity hound than the swaggering Johnson, and he was to be Matthew Webb's great rival – the Sebastian Coe to his Steve Ovett – but the strangest thing about this particular rivalry was that the man wasn't even a swimmer.

In sport, a good opponent can bring out the best in a man; the existence of a close rival focuses attention on technique, piles on the pressure, and the constant threat of being beaten keeps ambition burning. In an ideal world, a man would choose his rival, selecting him as carefully as he would a friend but, in reality, circumstance makes the decision for him. If, on leaving the Merchant Service, Webb had returned to Watson and become part of the amateur or professional swimming scenes, if he'd learned and practised the new overarm stroke and trained with a coach to develop speed to add to his natural stamina, if he'd matched himself against Parker, Johnson and young Willie Beckwith, then perhaps he would have become another such champion. His status would have grown as the sport matured, he might have become a member of the group which formed on 7 January 1879 to promote and improve competitive swimming and which later became the still existing and highly respected Amateur Swimming Association. He might have become a teacher of swimming and a winner of medals, but a fluke of timing meant that Webb's lifelong rival was a brave, cocksure American with a heart full of wanderlust, a talent for press relations, a wealthy backer and a keen eye to the main chance. His name was Paul Boyton – he called himself a captain but there is no evidence that he had any real claim to the rank – and he rode to fame on an extraordinary invention, launched under the uncatchy name of Merriman's Patent Waterproof Life-Saving Apparatus.

The eccentric Victorian inventor is such a stereotype in fiction that it comes as quite a shock to realise that he must have been based on real people. C. S. Merriman was an inventor and an entrepreneur from Iowa who, horrified by the multiple deaths resulting from the shipwreck of a pleasure boat, put his mind to life-saving. His Patent Waterproof Life-Saving Apparatus consisted of a tunic and trouser combination, rather like a Victorian woman's bathing costume, only made of black vulcanised rubber. The trousers covered the feet and were held up by braces. Around the waist of the trousers was a steel hoop to which the upper tunic was attached. The tunic had a hood and gloves were also provided, leaving the face as the only part of the body to remain uncovered. There were two layers to the suit and between them were the five all-important air chambers, two in the tunic chest, one around each leg from the hip to the knee and one in the hood, which were inflated by means of tubes, transforming the baggy suit into a tight-fitting rubber sausage. The entire dress weighed about 35 lb and was strong enough to support a weight of up to 300 lb. A large rubber bag was added with enough space for: 10 days' worth of food; a gallon of fresh water; signal lights; a small lamp like a miner's lamp, which could be attached to the head for night paddling; an axe for killing swordfish and a bowie knife for fighting off sharks; and, in case of boredom, books! Should you have the bad luck to find yourself on a capsizing boat, the idea was that you put on Merriman's suit – he claimed it took only 58 seconds to do so – and, when you hit the water, you assumed a horizontal position and steered yourself towards land with a six-foot-long double-bladed paddle; an optional sail could be attached to an iron hook on the feet. All in all, it was very odd-looking indeed. The suit had elements that would be familiar to a modern deep-sea diver, a kayaker would handle the paddles with ease, a windsurfer would appreciate the sail – and a fetishists' convention would open its doors to the wearer! As a sedentary businessman, Merriman knew he couldn't demonstrate his suit, and he was looking round for someone to do it for him.

The son of a travelling salesman who specialised in maritime curiosities, Paul Boyton was born in Allegheny, Pennsylvania and, by his own admission, had been a troublesome boy, the sort who likes to run away from home and hang around in gangs. Neither his mother's orders nor the laws of his home city had stopped him from bathing illegally in the local river.

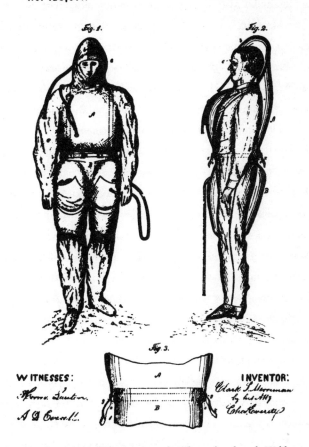

C. S. MERRIMAN.

. Improvement in Life-Preserving Dresses.

No. 128,971.   Patented July 16, 1872.

Fig. 1.   Fig. 2.

Fig. 3.

WITNESSES: INVENTOR:

Merriman's suit helped Boyton cross the Channel and made Webb determined to use only muscle power.

He was only a year younger than Webb and, like him, he had from an early age loved the water, a quality which made the Navy his first choice of career. But while Matthew Webb entered the Merchant Service, thrived within its structures and steadily climbed its hierarchy, Boyton's naval career was short, consisting of less than a year fighting the Confederates in the Southern States before leaving and setting off on seemingly aimless travels. His father found him a position on a boat bound for the West Indies on a collecting mission to bring home all kinds of marine curiosities. It was, in effect, an attempt to introduce Paul into the family business, but the boat sank off Barbados and Boyton decided not to return home, and threw in his lot with the Mexican revolutionaries. Quite why, he never attempted to explain. It's unlikely it was commitment to the cause of rejecting the emperor imposed on them by Napoleon III; the moment he realised they were in retreat, he left them and headed back to New York, arriving there at the beginning of June 1867. A period of relative calm followed after he agreed to his father's suggestion that he open a shop selling oriental goods by the sea in Cape May. But two years later, a fire burnt down both premises and goods and his father died, and the two events seemed to trigger in him a new zest for travel. He promptly set off for France where he volunteered to join the French Army to fight in the Franco-Prussian war. Once again that was only temporary. Subsequent adventures – to call them jobs doesn't do them justice – included a six-month stint as a submarine diver and a disastrous spell in South Africa where he'd been lured by stories about the vast fortunes to be found in the diamond mines. He didn't make a fortune and ended up hospitalised with a nasty leg injury. On his recovery, he returned to America. It was a miserable journey home; the ship's crew mutinied.

Boyton was, in short, a soldier of fortune, a gun for hire and just the sort of person who abandons a secure job to try his hand at promoting a new, untried invention. He would have seen no contradiction in being reckless in the cause of life-saving. When Merriman met him, he was in his mid-20s, a strong, healthy, athletic figure, 5 ft 10 in tall and 12 stone. He was brave, adventurous and a strong swimmer, with masses of energy and a passionate commitment to life-saving. He had been running the life-saving service at Atlantic City, a busy seaside resort near Philadelphia, for two years and his system was so efficient that he'd reduced the number of deaths by drowning from 20 per year to none. He had a high opinion of himself and the importance of his work. Once, when a man he'd rescued offered him a 50-cent note, he gave him 49 cents change and said: 'I could not think of taking a cent more than your life is worth.' Merriman thought the best, most newsworthy place to test his invention was the English Channnel and Boyton agreed. He was the sort of man of whom people say: 'He'll try anything once.'

Unlike Webb whose swimming ambitions were, at this stage, genuinely sportsmanlike, Boyton's were those of a man of business; To call his interest in the Channel commercial is not to criticise him;

'Captain' Paul Boyton,
as he appeared on the
frontispiece of
his autobiography.

his suit may look silly to modern eyes but deaths at sea were terrifyingly frequent in the 19th century, and life-saving was a serious issue for anyone who owned, sailed, chartered or simply stepped on board a boat. To attempt the Channel in Merriman's apparatus required strength and courage and Boyton had plenty of both, but none the less a paddling, windsurfing, rubber-suit-wearer, buoyed up by air cushions and protected from cold and wet, is an odd rival for a breast-stroker, supported only by his muscles and with his body totally open to the elements. It was nonsense to speak of them in the same breath but sport and spectacle were closely entwined and both men attempted the Channel in 1875 and within months of each other. That coincidence led the press, the public and the men themselves to regard themselves as opponents. It did Boyton no harm but, by accepting the rivalry, by forcing himself to live up to that challenge, Webb was to do terrible damage to his health and reputation.

Boyton soon became as enthusiastic about the Patent Waterproof Life-Saving Apparatus as Merriman could have wished. He wrote in his autobiography that his passion for life-saving 'amounted to a craze'. He was convinced that the suit could save thousands of lives and 'with the confidence of youth and the strength of manhood he was willing to take any chances to attain this object'. He spent hours practising in it and, together, he and Merriman planned a programme of demonstrations in and around New York. Boyton would paddle himself around on the water, letting off signal flares and occasionally lighting a cigar. Initial public response was underwhelming – the apparatus seems to have been regarded as mildly interesting but not worthy of serious attention – and Boyton's declaration that he would sail 200 miles out to sea from New York, don his suit, drop overboard and paddle back to shore was greeted with derision. He couldn't find a single ship's captain who would agree to carry him, and Boyton and Merriman's Patent Waterproof Life-Saving Apparatus were in danger of becoming a laughing stock.

Undaunted, on 11 October 1874 Paul Boyton boarded the steamer ship, the *Queen*, this time keeping quiet about his intentions. In the middle of the night, he was caught at the side of the ship, fully dressed in his suit, the air chambers already inflated and with his paddle at the ready. The furious captain ordered him seized and the suit confiscated; no such mad enterprise was going to start off from *his* ship. It says much for Boyton's eloquence and his confidence in the suit that the captain eventually agreed to put him overboard two and a half miles (much more realistic than the proposed 200) from the coast of Ireland and let him try his luck. He warned him that the storms would be fierce and the Irish coast nothing but steep cliffs so that, all in all, it would be better to give up. But Boyton was insistent. 'As I have promised I will stand by it,' he replied.

The steamer carrying news of the mad American reached Ireland long before Boyton. By the time he arrived, battered but unbroken by a 15-hour battle with waves that seemed at times to be 100 feet high, the Irish newspapers had already put reporters on the look out. Boyton had been almost blinded by the salt water, he'd feared for his life but, on stumbling ashore just south of Baltimore, he paused only to thank 'the great Pilot above' before heading to the nearest post office to send a telegram to the captain of the *Queen* and the *New York Herald*. Business was business after all – and his business was publicity.

This time the public response was all that he and Merriman could have wished for. By the time he'd reached Cork, he was famous. The *Cork Examiner* called his appearance the 'sensation of the day'. His hotel lobby was crammed with people craning to catch a glimpse of him; he was followed everywhere he went. It seemed all Ireland wanted to see the enterprising American and his amazing apparatus. He put on a show in Queenstown harbour and so many people wanted to attend that the Cork and Passage Railway Company laid on a special steamer to take spectators to his exhibition. For a huge and appreciative audience, he laid on his American show, paddling around for about an hour, eating and drinking, letting off signal flares and using the bowie knife to knock the tops off lemonade bottles. The novelty-hunting manager of the Opera Company at Munster promptly made him an offer: if he would appear in his suit in between the acts of the opera and talk about his adventures, the manager would give him half the house's takings and pay for the advertising. Paul accepted; he was spending money freely and so was glad to accept more and more offers to perform. He moved on to Dublin and charmed a large crowd of onlookers with an hour-long display of paddling, setting off rockets and cigar-smoking. Appearances followed at Dublin theatres, the zoological gardens and in the River Liffey. He was invited to meet Queen Victoria and Princess Beatrice on their yacht off the Isle of Wight where, despite being clad from head to toe in black rubber himself, he couldn't contain his surprise at the sight of Her Majesty's Highland servant, John Brown, in his kilt.

He paddled past the Dublin law courts, bringing the proceedings to a halt while barristers, solicitors and petitioners gazed out of the window. One day he literally stopped traffic; the tram cars braking to allow sightseers a better view. For his indoor performances he devised a special tableau: he would put on the suit,

attach the American flag to his paddle and a bucket of water would
be thrown over him. By the time he left Dublin at the end of 1874,
the newspapers were claiming that over 100,000 people had seen
his shows; that the newspapers now referred to the rubber suit as
the Boyton Suit might have annoyed Merriman but he could hardly
complain that nobody had noticed it. But sell-out performances,
the cheers of the crowd and meeting royalty were not enough for
Boyton. Ireland was flatteringly impressed but his mission – and
Merriman's too – was still to introduce the suit to Europe.
Christmas 1874 found Boyton in bed with a nasty fever, contracted
in the notoriously filthy waters of the River Liffey, but in the New
Year, while Webb was taking up his last Merchant Service position,
the captaincy of the *Emerald,* Boyton was convalescent and writing
to *The Times* newspaper from the American Exchange in Charing
Cross. He used the recent sinking of the ship *Cospatrick* with all its
passengers to draw attention to the usefulness of Merriman's Patent
Waterproof Life-Saving Apparatus. Boyton wrote in a highly stirring
prose which, if his speaking style was similar, accounts for the
popularity of his lectures. His depiction of the terrified *Cospatrick*
passengers was masterly: 'In the awful solitude of mid-ocean whole
families are roused in the dead of night from their hopeful dreams
of a promised land to be swept struggling into eternity, nothing left
them in their last brief hour of agony but the choice of suffocation,
either by the devouring flames or the merciless billows.' The solution
to all this, he went on, was Merriman's Patent Waterproof Life-

Saving Apparatus, 'unquestionably, the greatest, as it is the best, life-preserver in existence'. The editor of *The Times* letters page was clearly impressed as he allocated the writer the best part of a column.

In March, Boyton was back in *The Times*, this time as the subject, when he and two other gentlemen demonstrated the rubber suit in the Thames. Almost as a throwaway line came the amazing statement that 'he purposes making a voyage from Dover to Calais as soon as his arrangements permit'. All this must have made Webb feel sick with fury and alarm. 'The man is an obvious fraud,' he would always say of Boyton, but it looked as if the obvious fraud would still get there before him. The Channel would not be warm enough to swim in until the summer, and anyway his savings had run out and he had to go back to sea. In January, he took up the captaincy of the *Emerald* and left England on what would be his last voyage. He would be away for months, leaving the path clear for Boyton. He knew there was no way that Boyton's efforts would go unnoticed; in choosing the Channel, Boyton had unerringly picked the body of water best calculated to capture the British imagination.

Chapter 4

A Mere Ditch That Shall Be Leaped

The idea of swimming the Channel, and showing practically as it were what a very narrow 'silver streak' divides us from our neighbours, has for many years exercised the minds of those who have devoted themselves to the art of natation and attained great proficiency in it.

——— The Standard, *26 August 1875*

The story of the Channel is the story of England. There is scarcely a key event in English history, at least in popular history, the kind that features in children's books and stays in the adult imagination, turning the past into a series of dates, battles and glorious events, where the Channel does not appear. It saw Caesar come ashore at Walmer and Deal in 55 BC and it supposedly soaked Canute's toes on the beach at Southampton when it demonstrated that, powerful though he was, he was not the sea's master. William the Conqueror and his 12,000 men crossed it in 1066 and landed at Pevensey Bay before beginning the most famous battle in British history.

It is Shakespeare's 'silver sea', his 'moat defensive to a house', and with the sinking of the Armada, it became the grave of Spanish hopes of invasion. For Napoleon, it was a 'mere ditch that shall be leaped when one is daring enough to try', and it saw the last of the humiliated emperor when he was imprisoned on the ship *Bellerephon* and anchored off Torbay before he made his long final journey to St Helena.

Its original name was Oceanus Britannicus; the French call it La Manche; to mariners of the past it was the Narrow Seas and to the world in general it is the English Channel, except in the lexicon of long-distance swimmers when it is simply the Channel. The one and only Channel.

A 350-mile strip of salt water, it stretches from the Scilly Isles in the west, up past the Dover Straits in the east. At its widest, it is 112 miles and between Dover in Kent and Cap Gris Nez near Calais, only 21, so narrow that on a clear day you can see the coast of France from the English shore. It's not particularly deep, ranging from 400 feet right up to 150 feet. If St Paul's Cathedral were to be sunk at its shallowest point, its dome would appear above the surface.

It is frighteningly unpredictable being the shifting, often violent meeting point for the icy waters which have passed round the north of Scotland on their way east and south, and the mighty Atlantic as it sweeps up the Channel. It has a tidal system so complex only an experienced sailor can understand it and sea conditions so wayward that the only thing you can say for sure is that you can never be quite sure what they will be. Spend a holiday on the Channel coastline and the odds are against you enjoying three days of good weather in a row. More ships have been sunk in the Channel than in any other equivalent area in the world. Over £2,000m worth of shipping lies on the treacherous Goodwin Sands, a 12-mile long by two-mile wide sand bank, nicknamed the 'ship-swallower'.

It was this mysterious, frightening, ancient piece of England that Johnson had aspired to, Boyton had come to claim and Webb was forced to wait for.

In the second week of April 1875, Boyton checked into the Lord Warden Hotel in Dover. His entourage included his older brother, various friends, the suit's inventor, C. S. Merriman, and about 20 English, French and American newspapermen. So many people wanted to see his attempted crossing that he had to charter a steamer to accommodate them all. Boyton was in good spirits; he'd received a letter expressing support from General Schench, the United States minister, and he was aware that Captain Bruce, the Admiralty superintendent in Dover, was standing by to telegraph the details of his crossing to Queen Victoria at Osborne House.

Daring though the venture was, plenty of attention was paid to safety. Two doctors – the local Dr Diver and Mr Willis, a London surgeon – travelled in the steamer and the Boulogne Humane

Society sent a small sailing boat and a rowing boat to accompany Boyton. More attention should perhaps have been paid to his starting time. Boyton seems to have entrusted that decision to the pilot of the Boulogne Humane Society boat and a few old salts from Dover. Their theory was that he should enter the water at three o'clock on the morning of 10 April and attempt to catch the tide as it pushed east up the Channel. It sounded fine in theory but it depended on a punctual start and Boyton maintaining the correct speed to catch the tide as it turned.

He was late for the most farcical reason; he was wearing thicker stockings than normal and it took him longer to squeeze into his rubber suit. As a result, three o'clock came and went and found him still in the hotel. More time was wasted making his way through the crowds in the harbour. Neither his friends nor the newspaper reporters had bothered to get any sleep, instead spending the waiting hours in the hotel parlour and the town of Dover had clearly decided to stay up and party too. If a rousing send-off was what Boyton wanted, he had no cause for complaint. The gas lights flared, rockets lit the sky and bonfires blazed.

Standing on Admiralty Pier, Boyton inflated his suit and prepared to depart. He was carrying his paddle, a fog horn, a flask of brandy, a bowie knife and a packet of letters entitled 'the Boyton mail for the Continent'. A gun on a boat at anchor in the Channel blasted out, announcing his start, a full 20 minutes later than planned.

He made a poor beginning. He waded into the water but almost immediately the paddles of the tug began to revolve and the churning water whirled Boyton back against the landing stage. None the less he worked his paddles vigorously and finally got away. Just past the pier, the current caught him and moved him swiftly up the coast just as planned. At half past four, he attached a sail the size of a large handkerchief to his foot, at 5.20, he paused to cheer and wave at his supporters on the boat as they hoisted the stars and stripes, and at six o'clock, he lit himself a very fine cigar. The pilot declared that he was about eight miles from the English coast and that he could make out Cape Gris Nez in the distance. Two carrier pigeons were fitted with the good news and, after wheeling round the steamer for a few minutes, set off for their destination. The message was simply: 'All well.'

Three hours later, the good mood had diminished. Because of his late start, Boyton had missed the French current, he was complaining of tiredness, the weather had turned nasty and he was being buffeted cruelly by the waves. From the boat, Mr McGarahan, the *New York Herald* reporter saw the drama unfold: 'It was a strangely fascinating spectacle to watch him in his hand-to-hand struggle with the ocean. The waves seemed to become living things animated by a terrible hatred for the strange being battling with them. Sometimes they seemed to withdraw for a moment, as if by concert, and then rush down on him from all sides, roaring like wild beasts.'

At 9.20, Boyton removed his sail and took a rest in the water, holding on to the side of the boat, while he discussed the situation with his pilot and his brother. The pilot declared (erroneously as it turned out) that they were just 12 miles from France, and Boyton was still sure that he could make it. He paddled on – no one ever doubted his courage – but, by one o'clock, when he stopped for a gulp of cherry brandy, instead of being several miles south of Boulogne, he was almost opposite and the current had again turned against him. All through that afternoon, the weather grew worse; it was cold and rainy and there was a thick fog settling down over Boyton and the boat. At half past five, another consultation revealed the pilot and the captain of the tug hopelessly divided on Boyton's position. They both had opinions about how far Boyton still had to go but it was evident by now that neither could be relied on. Some things were easy to understand, though: there was no land in sight and the wind and sea were rising. Tempers flared, Boyton's brother insisting that he be allowed to continue, the captain of the tug saying equally firmly that he wouldn't risk his men's lives and the pilot declaring that once darkness fell, he could no longer take responsibility for Boyton's safety. His brother finally agreed to tell Boyton he should leave the water, since the suit had proved its efficacy and the weather was too bad to continue.

At first Boyton refused. It was only when convinced that they were basically lost at sea that he yielded. Even then, he paddled once around the steamer to show that he was strong enough to continue before coming on deck, grumbling that it was not his choice. He had been in the water for 15 hours. Dr Diver examined him as he lay wrapped in a blanket and pronounced him 'calm and collected. He showed no visible signs of distress, apart from being a little sulky. He was perspiring freely and his respiration was perfectly normal; pulse 80 and feeble; temperature 97 and a trace.' The pilot and the captain finally worked out their position and headed for Boulogne. On their arrival, Boyton once again dressed himself in his life-saving outfit and went ashore, still insisting that he could easily have paddled for another 10 hours.

From the excitement and furore that followed, anyone might be forgiven for thinking that Boyton had actually succeeded. He received a telegram which stated that 'Her Majesty had received the news of Captain Boyton's safe arrival at Boulogne with much pleasure and congratulated him on the success of his expedition.' The Lord Mayor of London applauded 'the success which he had achieved so gallantly in the interests of humanity'. The Boulogne Humane Society might have sent him an inadequate pilot but Boyton was still pleased to receive a gold medal from them and praise for his services to humanity. He delivered a lecture in the Hall of the Établissement des Bains, and his two-hour display of his life-saving suit in Boulogne harbour was watched by 20,000 spectators. All in all, his crossing, though incomplete, was excellent publicity. Within days, he'd embarked on a full schedule of engagements. Three days of exhibitions in Birmingham earned him over £600.

But the Channel has a way of getting under a man's skin and, at the end of May, Boyton was in France, looking again at the cold, green, tempting stretch of water and planning another crossing. He never explained why he decided to start from France this time but it was a good idea as it is now known that the France to England crossing is easier than the other way. England has about four miles of coastline which is more or less the same distance from Cap Gris Nez. Going the other way, missing the prominent Cap, adds an extra mile to your swim. Plus, there are currents which push swimmers *away* from the French shore. Other factors remained the same, however. Once again, he started at three o'clock in the morning and once again, his departure was a flashy affair. A rocket announced the start, a display of fireworks answered the rocket.

His second attempt was as smooth as his first was rocky. The first fine mist of the morning lifted and by six o'clock, he'd paddled himself five miles out from the French coast. Four hours later, sail and paddle combined brought him almost to the middle of the Channel. At 11 o'clock, strong green tea and a few rounds of beef sandwiches made an excellent breakfast and he sailed and paddled on. At a quarter past midday, the white cliffs of Dover emerged from the haze and a steamboat full of day-trippers waved their handkerchiefs and cheered; Captain Boyton hoisted the American flag by way of response. After four p.m., the flood tide began to sweep him towards the English shore and he was only six miles from

Dover as night began to fall around six p.m. At nine o'clock he had more beef sandwiches and tea, sure now that success was in sight; the current was carrying him in. He couldn't have asked for a more peaceful crossing; the only incident of note came around one o'clock in the morning when a porpoise startled him. By two a.m., he was so close to his destination that, in the words of one observer, 'one might almost throw a biscuit ashore'. At half past two, to the sound of a triumphant rocket blast from his accompanying boat, he landed on a rocky strip of beach in Fan Bay. He was elated and smiling, warmed by hot blankets and the praise of friends and supporters. A doctor who examined him pronounced him to be in good condition; Boyton later declared: 'Money could not bribe me to undertake the trip again.'

As the telegraph system and the press did their work, Boyton found himself inundated with praise. Telegrams arrived at the Pavillion Hotel constantly. There was one from the Queen – Her Majesty was 'much pleased to hear the news' – and 'cordial congratulations' from the Prince of Wales. There were banquets in Dover and Folkestone; Boyton's health was drunk, his suit admired and everyone laughed at his jokes and applauded him when he said that money was not his object but service to humanity. Within a week, Boyton was back on the exhibition trail. He travelled all over England, charging 50 guineas a day to appear and display his suit. Only the *Daily Telegraph* sounded a sour note. While praising Boyton's 'undaunted courage and energy', it also wondered:

Boyton in his
life-saving suit.

'Whether the invention is ever likely to be of any marked practical use no one can at present tell.'

But the sniffiness of the *Daily Telegraph* was nothing compared to the outright contempt felt by Matthew Webb. He never spoke of Boyton with anything less than derision and liked to joke: 'Boyton's dress was in the cause of humanity, but a man could not always be having it on – he would look so.'

It feels uncharitable to deny Boyton his success, for it was short-lived indeed. In June of that year, while the ink was barely dry on the triumphant newspaper stories, Captain Matthew Webb left the Merchant Service and prepared to make his own crossing.

He was now 27 and all signs of the undersized child had disappeared. He was 5 ft 8½ in tall, with thick muscles, broad shoulders and strong arms and legs. He had grown a thick moustache and his blue eyes looked out of the red, leathery face of someone naturally pale-skinned who has spent a lot of time outdoors in hot countries. He left the Service with a good reputation; he was a somebody, having reached the top of his profession with a salary of at least 13s 6d a day. Assuming he spent on average 10 months a year at sea, he could expect to earn an annual salary of £205. It wasn't a fortune – a professional man earned around £500 a year – but at sea, he wouldn't have had to pay for his accommodation and food. He had commanded men – the captain's word was law on board ship – and learned discipline – both how to obey and how to make others obey. He was known for competence and bravery, but a certain unpredictable streak, a tendency to surprise and disturb also marked him out. As captain, he had a reputation for fast passages, making him popular with his employers. By his crew, however, he was less liked. Many who signed on with him once never did so again. Daring and a reckless disregard for one's own safety are inspiring qualities, but caution and an appreciation of other people's fears are, understandably, preferred by ships' crews.

Despite the grumblings of former crew members, his career had been a success. Moreover, it had given him three things: an outlet for his restless spirit, enough time and opportunity to master sea swimming and the pair of bright-red regulation *Conway* bathing trunks which he wore when he swam the Channel.

In June 1875, he moved to London, took up his lodgings in Poplar and got back in touch with Beckwith and Watson. Between them, they moved fast. The Channel swim had to take place in the next couple of months; any later than August and the sea would drop well below 60 degrees Fahrenheit, becoming much too cold for the human body to stand.

Webb began to train at the Lambeth Baths again, under the tutoring eye of the professor. Beckwith wanted him to learn the faster side stroke and, although he always preferred breast stroke, he did master it. The Lambeth Baths were always busy, as Beckwith gathered round himself an odd assortment of swimmers and gymnasts, writers and sporting baronets who liked to bet on races. Through Watson and Beckwith, Webb got to know a new set of people, wholly unlike the professional men of his provincial childhood or the sailors he'd worked with. His new friends were sophisticated metropolitan men, men who were good with words, who spoke and wrote wittily, who enjoyed late nights and good dinners with jolly toasts and long talks. Men like Frank Buckland, the owner and editor of a weekly paper called *Land and Water*. Buckland was a lover of the active, the physical, the natural and the unusual. He filled *Land and Water* with stories about new arrivals at the Natural History Museum, discussions about salmon fishing and pictures of unusual creatures such as the manatee, the great sea cow. One of his best writers, Arthur Payne, was a swimmer and he took a keen interest in Webb. A Cambridge man, he was also a rower, a skilled billiards player and an excellent cook. Then there was Charles 'Boy' Baker, a brilliant young swimmer and great diver, and Henry Wilkinson who was a member of the Ilex Swimming Club and a friend of Payne. Among all these unfamiliar faces, Webb rediscovered a family member, George Ward, a distant cousin, who later became Webb's brother-in-law when he married his younger sister, Sarah.

Beckwith, Watson and Webb formed a sociable triumvirate. They swam together, drank together and chased women together. There were always girls hanging round the swimming races and, as Watson coyly recalled, he and Webb enjoyed 'very pleasant conversation' with them. One such evening chat resulted in the two men being drenched in a thunderstorm that burst as they tramped home in the dark after an interlude in a 'secluded thoroughfare'. They liked practical jokes, Watson and Webb once locking Beckwith out of his hotel room and then Webb, stark naked, chasing the older man down the corridor.

By the beginning of July, Watson and Beckwith thought their new swimmer was ready for his first public outing. He was still slow but, over a distance, he was exceptional. There was a long-standing bet lodged at *Bell's Life* magazine which invited any man to try his luck swimming from Brunswick Pier in Blackwall to Tower Pier in Gravesend, and Webb declared that he would try for it. For £10 at odds of two to one, he would complete the 18-mile swim without touching the boat or any other person or – a sideswipe at Boyton? – using 'any life-saving dress or artificial means of floating'. There was only one taker, but the early afternoon sun of Saturday 3 July found Webb in Blackwall, stripped and ready to swim. A steamboat, the *Falcon*, was chartered to follow him, Robert Watson was umpire, Professor Beckwith steered him from a small boat and Willie Beckwith was on hand to dive in and rescue Webb if he needed it.

It was a good choice of swim. It took the swimmer along the Thames, maximising the number of people who would see him; it was long, but the swimmer would have the tide with him and, therefore, it was a lot easier than it appeared. He had a good day for it too; the Thames, though as usual an open sewer, was unusually smooth.

Thanks in no small part to the fast-flowing river, Webb moved quickly away from the pier. Within 40 minutes of starting, he was passing the pier at Charlton near Greenwich and was cheered by the young sailors on board a training ship moored nearby. From there, he picked up his pace a little and did the next three and a half miles in 45 minutes. He was attracting plenty of attention; several boats were now following him and there was much shouting and pointing. Webb and the river swept on to Woolwich. Here, the sun went down and it began to rain heavily but Webb took no notice and swam on. He was disturbed by the disgusting water at Crossness but swam through it and four o'clock found him treading water and drinking brandy from a flask handed to him by young Beckwith. Willie then stripped off his own clothes and joined Webb in the dirty water, swimming alongside him for half a mile. On and on they went, the tireless swimmer, the watchful boat and the flowing Thames, past Erith Pier, past the isolated tavern on Long Beach where the prize fighters drank and Webb now paused to eat some bread. Then on again, past Greenhithe, still moving strongly, the Thames moving with him, his strong arms and legs and the water combined to take him on round the point opposite Grays, past another training ship with cheering boys, alongside boats full of lads and ladies and an officer. At five past seven, he passed Rotherville Pier, lined with hundreds of cheering people; one more gulp from the flask of brandy and it was on, quietly, confidently, to Gravesend Pier which he reached at nearly 17 minutes past seven. He needed no help in climbing into the boat and seemed to his friends not much the worse for the exercise.

The press reports that followed were mixed. Some publications, like *Bell's Life* and *Land and Water*, chronicled the event in detail but without any extra gloss. The *Daily News*, on the other hand, was more enthusiastic, calling it a 'remarkable exhibition of natatory power and skill', and declared itself amazed: 'at first it would seem that the power of so small an object as one man in a vast expanse of water would be altogether inadequate', to cover such a distance. The *Globe* was less impressed. Calculating that, as the tide runs at four miles an hour and a man in the water would be carried along as fast as the tide (which he would not), it concluded that Webb had only swum one furlong, i.e. one eighth of a mile. As the swim had taken him four hours, 52 minutes and 44 seconds, the implication was that Webb was not a very good swimmer at all. That was the only mean-minded comment. The general feeling was that Webb had acquitted himself well. Backed by the powerful Beckwith, a friend of the knowledgeable Watson and the swimmer of a good distance, Webb was beginning to build a name for himself in the swimming fraternity. But, to his disgust, 'that fellow Boyton' had not gone away. On 13 July, the American was writing once again to *The Times,* drawing attention to himself by complaining about the condition of the water in the River Calder in Wakefield. Three days later the same paper noted his presence at a grand fête in Lake Windermere. For a while longer, Webb must be content mainly with notices in the sporting press. And readers of the 17 July issues of *Bell's Life* and *Land and Water* would have seen the following:

> I am authorised by Captain Webb to announce his full
> determination to attempt the feat of swimming across the
> Channel. Captain Webb, who has gone to Dover and
> commenced training, says the distance is but 18 miles. He
> can swim one mile and a half in an hour, and can remain

in the water 14 hours. By choosing therefore a hot day, when the tide is slack, he argues that the feat, at any rate, is possible. Beyond a paltry £20 to £1, he has nothing to gain by success. Surely, under the circumstances, there are some lovers of sport who would gladly, in sporting language, 'put him on so much to nothing'. Should he by chance succeed, which is extremely improbable, it would be cruel that one who would undoubtedly have performed the greatest athletic feat on record should be a loser by the event.

It was signed by Webb's friend, Payne.

The 'paltry bet' so derided by Payne came from a Mr Rawden, who wrote to take up the challenge but displayed a cautious nature by adding: 'provided that you have indisputable proof that the event of the feat, during the present season, being said to be accomplished, it really was'. He probably thought he was being very generous when he stated: 'Should the swimmer succeed in his project I shall not regret the loss of the money.'

Payne then attempted to push up the betting by sounding a note of doubt in parenthesis: 'We have so little belief in the practicability of the feat that we have no hesitation in offering to bet Captain Webb £50 to nothing against it . . . We once stayed in the sea two hours, swimming from Shakespeare Cliff to Folkestone, and found the water of the Channel much colder than in the Thames. We do not believe in any man being able to swim more than one mile an hour for any length of time in the sea.' But, he added, Webb 'is a likely man to bear fatigue and cold, and we shall await with some interest the attempt, and should he succeed we will cheerfully lose our £50'.

Indoor training can help you build up speed and correct any faults in your stroke but it cannot prepare you for long-distance swimming nor toughen your body against cold. So, just over a fortnight after his Blackwall to Gravesend swim, Webb went down to Dover and reacquainted himself with the Channel by swimming east up the Kent coast to Ramsgate, a distance of 20 miles and a course where he would have, for some of the time at least, the tide against him. Dover, despite attempts to make it into a coastal resort as jolly as Brighton, has always been a place of departure and a certain melancholy hangs over the town. Webb went alone, he made all his arrangements alone, hiring a local boatman, William Cole, and arranging for a reporter from the *Dover Chronicle* to accompany him.

The morning of Monday 19 July was completely wrong for a swim in the sea. It was raining heavily and sensible holidaymakers would have been snuggled beside the fire in their hotels, wishing they'd picked another week for their annual holiday. There was no crowd of onlookers at the Admiralty Pier, no cheers, no team spirit, just three men each with a job to do. In the pouring rain, Webb stripped and rubbed his body with cod liver oil.

They started just before 10 o'clock, Webb swimming rapidly with the tide, his face set against the rain, the reporter and Cole alongside him in a small boat. First breast stroke, then on his side, then breast stroke again, but always maintaining a slow, steady pace of about 20 strokes to the minute. It was monotonous work. For more than two and a half hours, Webb swam through the rain and the sea, pausing only once to gulp down a quarter-pint of ale which the drenched men on the boat handed to him; the salt water was making him thirsty, he said. At 20 minutes to one, he'd gone half the distance and still the rain kept falling, but he was swimming steadily, not showing any signs of being weary. A few miles past Deal, the tide began to pull from Sandwich Haven and Cole directed him away from it. Then he was past Sandwich and making for Ramsgate, moving more slowly now, fighting against the tide which was ebbing away from Ramsgate Pier. He seemed to be swimming like an automaton; nothing in his face suggested tiredness. To every enquiry about his condition, he answered cheerfully: 'All right.'

At last, with Ramsgate Pier just feet away, the sun came out to smile on him. There was a small welcoming committee on the pier, a few cheers with Cole egging them on. 'Give another one,' he shouted, 'for he deserves it.' Just after half past six, Webb climbed up the ladder on to the pier to receive the congratulations of the Ramsgate harbour master. It was a quiet arrival, just a rub-down in front of the fire in the harbour master's office and then out to dinner.

Once again, his swim was ignored by the national newspapers. *The Times* preferred to cover in detail yet another of Boyton's appearances. After all, they probably reasoned, Boyton was on the Thames; newspapers have never been anything other than parochial and London-based tends to mean London-biased. Even locally, the swim was something of a damp squib. Only the *Dover Chronicle* covered it, the town's other newspaper preferring to give space to Boyton's display of paddle-working and American flag-flying. At that point, it seems, Boyton was a guaranteed news story, Webb little more than a summer-season prankster with the ghost of Johnson's failure malignantly haunting his attempt.

Back in London, Webb visited King's College Hospital to have a full physical check-up. He was examined by Dr Henry Smith whose report was printed in *Land and Water*. There is something disquieting about the report, a voyeuristic and lubricious quality in the detailed description of Matthew Webb's physique:

He weighed, stripped, 14 st 8 lb; height 5 ft 8 in; age 27 years. Girth round chest, tight measurement over nipples, with arms up, 40½ in round the waist, just touching the lower rib, and three-and-a-half inches above the navel, 35½ in. This gave a very good relative proportion, showing that his large chest capacity is constant from top to bottom, and that the upper measurement is not due to any abnormal development of

muscle . . . His chest is deep without the slightest
tendency to pigeon-breast. His legs are straight and well
set on a substantial pelvis, with a firm but by no means
undue development of the gluteus maximus . . . Webb,
therefore, I should say, would never be a very fast
swimmer from the size and weight of his loins and legs,
but this weight means in the long run reserve force . . .
The Sartorius muscles which nip the legs together and
tend greatly to produce that long propelling leg action
are firm and large. Webb would undoubtedly make a
good wrestler . . . and might prove a heavy hitter with
the gloves, but such continued slow action of the arms
from swimming during his life would be almost sure to
make him slow to lead or return. Round the arm, three
inches above elbow, he measures 13½ in, and round the
fore-arm 2½ in, below elbow 11¼ in; owing to the
quantity of flesh upon his arms the outlines of the triceps
and deltoid are not clearly defined.

Dr Smith, after applying the stethoscope, described the sounds of
the heart as perfectly healthy, and breathing remarkably clear and
full in the lungs in front and behind; though Webb once had a slight
attack of inflammation of the lungs it had left no trace.

What this report tells us is that Webb was slightly chubby and
that, in sporting circles, he was being regarded in much the same

way as a racehorse would be. Perhaps he felt comfortable with that sort of attention; he certainly doesn't seem to have objected. It is likely that, by that stage, he was thinking only of the swim ahead of him with the sort of concentrated single-mindedness that blots out the irrelevant and the trivial. But, whether he was aware of it or not, a blueprint for his future was being drawn up, he was being showcased, turned into an exhibit. He certainly received no practical help from the doctor.

He had another visit to pay before he left town – to Frank Buckland at *Land and Water*. Buckland had two things to offer: a jar of porpoise oil for greasing his body to keep out the cold and some lavish advice on the best diet to follow during the swim. Had Webb been looking for the heaviest, hardest to digest, most nauseating foods possible, it might have been useful. 'A very moderate use of brandy,' was Buckland's suggestion. 'Strong beef tea, rich glutinous soup, such as good mock turtle made from fat calves' head, and not pigs' head as is too often the case, strong hot coffee, or even, if possible, a good slice of juicy meat with a little stale bread . . . An egg beat up with a little sherry, or any form of concentrated nourishment . . . a lump of Liebig's extract of meat occasionally might be beneficial, mixed with dripping.'

Webb took the oil but very wisely ignored the dietary advice. He left London early in August, moved down to Dover where he lived at the Flying Horse Hotel, gradually acclimatising his body to the Channel. His training regime was simple and he followed it rigorously, paying as much attention to conserving his strength as he did to building it up. Every day he swam for about an hour in the sea and then, every tenth day, he took a long swim of up to four or five hours. He ate three meals a day, breakfast, dinner and tea, the last two consisting of meat containing a lot of fat and salad. He gave up tea and coffee, drank no spirits, just three pints of beer a day. After his tea, which was always at eight p.m., he took a walk in the fresh air for an hour before going to bed at exactly 10 o'clock.

Nowadays if you wanted to swim the Channel, you would ring the Channel Swimming Association and they would direct you to a pilot, experienced in guiding swimmers across. And you would quickly find yourself part of a group of men and women wanting to swim the Channel who would gather together to train throughout the spring and summer months. And there would be people around to give you advice, people who knew what they were talking about, who'd swum the Channel themselves or who'd witnessed dozens of crossings, people whose training and dietary theories were based on sound medical principles, who knew how to take boats and swimmers across the Channel: in short, people who'd done it before. But, apart from Johnson's one hour in the water, this was the first serious Channel attempt, and everything Webb found out he was discovering for the first time. And the first thing he would have realised is that there's nothing like ignorance for producing experts.

The first problem was his route, and here the opinion among local boatmen and pilots was divided, though much ale was drunk and much time wasted in discussing it. One old sea dog thought the swim was a cinch: 'Lor' bless you, the captain can stop in a week, and when he comes out will stand steady while we scrape the barnacles off him.' Another said 'them tides' were impossible to cross. Despite his own experience as a sailor, Webb was pretty clueless about conditions in the Straits of Dover. He adopted Boyton's approach, deciding to start with the flood tide which ran to the east from the Dover shore and calculating that he would be far enough out to sea to catch the current when it turned west. He reckoned he could do the swim in 14 hours. He ignored the fact that this strategy had failed Boyton. How cold was the water in mid-Channel, he wanted to know? Colder than along the coast? If so, then his Dover to Ramsgate swim might not have prepared him – but nobody knew for certain. Would the sun in his eyes blind him? He was offered a pair of spectacles, or perhaps he could black round his eyes to throw off the glare?

Who would go with him? He decided on a lugger, a small, trim sailing boat which would be captained by its owner George Toms, a short, tough, serious-minded Dover man, and a crew of six including two of Toms' sons. The members of the press would make up the numbers. There would also be a small rowing boat with Boy Baker on board, wearing a life-belt, ready to rescue him. And they would take a stove and some bricks that could be warmed up for Webb and a thick blanket. There would be no doctor. He didn't want one, feeling sure that he knew his own strength best.

What foods should he eat? Again nobody knew for sure. In the end, the lugger was packed as if for a picnic. Hot coffee, beef tea, roast beef, sandwiches cut into small pieces for easy consumption in the water. There would also be plenty of ale and brandy, the former to quench his thirst, the latter to stimulate him on the last leg of the swim.

If you want to swim the Channel, you must first learn how to wait. The sea has two tides – neap one week, spring the next. The neap tides are much smaller and therefore the best choice for a swimmer, but if a neap coincides with bad weather and rough seas you will have to wait another fortnight. If you are an exceptionally strong swimmer and very confident, you might risk going at the lowest end of a spring tide, but it will probably be best to wait. So every day you scrutinise the sky for signs, you talk to experts, you ignore the doomsayers, you examine the barometer. You keep your fingers crossed and pray for fine weather – and you keep on waiting. It plays hell with your nerves.

Throughout the first week of August 1875, Dover saw nothing but grey, sulky skies and a sullen lumpen sea and Webb trained in the harbour every day and waited. A jellyfish stung him during one of his swims and made him feel sick for the rest of the day, but he rubbed his chest with cod liver oil and carried on swimming and waiting. Inside, he was a nervous wreck, later recalling: 'I had some little fear of being laughed at if I failed and dreaded the kindness and sympathy of my friends, especially at home, more even than the open ridicule of comparative strangers.' Publicly, he showed no doubts and no fear, walking about Dover with his head held high and his shoulders squared. He looked what he was, a man with his mind set on a purpose. He never spoke about the Channel voluntarily, never called it by name, and when other people introduced the subject, he would only talk about the forthcoming swim as his 'big job'. He admitted to being confident but by no means positive of success. 'If I don't get the whole of the distance, I shall get as far as I can,' he told one questioner. Another time he said: 'I shall not give up while I have strength to wag a finger.' When anyone pointed out to him the difficulties which Boyton had experienced, even in his life-saving suit – and many people did – he replied shortly: 'I don't know what Captain Boyton can do, I only know what I can do.' Sometimes he'd joke: 'I have an advantage over other men. I am Webb-footed.' But Dover boatmen, men who knew the sea between England and France, shook their heads and predicted certain failure.

Finally he decided on a day – Tuesday 10th, in the morning. But Tuesday morning came and the weather was still bad and so he went on waiting. Tomorrow, he said; but Wednesday morning was not much better and the evening saw the sea churning in the harbour. The following day, Thursday, the sea had calmed a little, though it was still lumpy and forbidding, but something seemed to snap in Webb. He would go that day. Perhaps he felt embarrassed with his friends and supporters kicking their heels in the hotel, watching him and watching the weather. More likely, he'd just had enough of the waiting and his overwrought nerves had twanged once too often and he wanted to be up and doing.

At 10 minutes to five that afternoon, Webb and his companions were ready in Dover Harbour. If Webb was alarmed by the recent thunderstorm that had created that growling sea, or the fact that it was chilly and getting dark and that the wind was whistling on his body, he gave no sign. Quite possibly he felt it was too late to turn back now. He'd rubbed himself well with Buckland's porpoise oil, eaten a light meal and felt healthy and keyed up. The plan was that he would walk from the beach to the Admiralty Pier and dive in from there but there were too many people on the pier so, instead, he climbed on to George Toms' lugger and sailed in it round to the end of the pier. The water there was running swiftly and the boat tipped with the ripple, unappealing conditions for a long swim, but Webb undressed quickly and dived in.

Chapter 5

Too Much Sea

There's a switch between your brain and your
body and when your body is screaming at you to
stop, when it's in pain, you've got to be able to
flick that switch so your brain doesn't listen to
that pain. You have to get into the frame of mind
where nothing matters except finishing.
_____ *Alison Streeter, 'Queen of the Channel', 1998*

The coldness of the water chills the dream and
petrifies the ambition.
_____ It's Cold in the Channel, *Sam Rockett, 1956*

Webb recorded his memories of that swim in his characteristically
laconic style:

I could hear the people cheering on the shore. But the
billows soon overflowed that pleasant sound, and seemed

to strike at one angrily. The tide turned against me after a little and the sea was getting so rough that the lugger which accompanied me could not keep close, but a small boat was with me. The waves were pretty rough, but as yet I got the best of them. I was not cold, but really cheerful, for I heard I had gone seven miles towards the French coast by nine o'clock. At ten the rain came down in torrents. It was so thick the lugger could not be seen, and it was only by burning blue lights that they could tell where we were. The sea was rising every minute, breaking over the small boat, and threatening to swamp it. It was making a shuttlecock of poor me, but I worked away and accomplished nine miles but the small boat suffered more than I did and those in it finally called out to me that they could stand it no longer. I was disappointed, for I was strong and hearty and had accomplished more than half the distance across. But there was no help for it, and at 11.45, after being in the water nearly seven hours, I got out into the boat, which reached the lugger after a hard pull, and I returned a beaten man – the elements were too strong for me that time.

This brief account doesn't do justice to the sheer awfulness of that crossing both for him and his friends. It doesn't mention how horrifying it was to see the fierce waves wash over him or how frustrating to glimpse the cliffs of Calais, gleaming white and tantalisingly near-looking but stubbornly beyond reach. It doesn't describe the terror of being thrown around on a rough sea in an open boat, lit only by one dim tallow candle lantern on a night so dark you can see less than two yards ahead. There is no mention of the heart-sickening lurch between hope – when the boatmen declared that the weather would settle – and disappointment – when the sea-wise George Toms pursed his lips and shook his head. Or of the seasickness that has you vomiting over the edge of the boat or crawling miserably to lie down somewhere and wish you were dead. Nearly all the reporters were sick, one could keep going only by gulping a large glass of brandy and another gave up the struggle and insisted on hitching a lift on a small boat that was heading back to Dover.

And to say that the 'rain came down in torrents' doesn't really explain just how thick and blinding it was and how the wind that came with it blew the boat away from the swimmer, making the sails flap and creak and shriek as the crew desperately tried to keep close to him but were beaten away.

Most of all, in Webb's account, we do not hear the dis-appointment and sense of failure in his voice that was so apparent to his friends. 'It's no use,' he said, 'There is too much sea on. I must turn it up.' They watched him swim alongside the small boat and climb in. Three minutes later, he was on board the lugger, the boat was drawn up and Toms was directing his crew to head for Calais with all speed. Webb drank a glass of ale, turned into a berth and went to sleep.

He was not a moment too soon. Fifteen minutes later, the sea was in such a rage that the boat would have been forced away from Webb and he would almost certainly have drowned. But, as Toms told him, in the inevitable post-mortem, he'd swum more than half-way across, and had he been luckier with the weather and perhaps started in daylight, would probably have made it. He and his crew were ready to try again whenever he was.

Webb returned to Dover and to waiting and watching, trying to stay simultaneously alert and relaxed. He consulted with George Toms daily. As a sailor himself, he recognised an expert when he met one and knew that his success would depend to a great extent on Toms' navigation. The pressure was enormous: he'd left the Merchant Service for this, he was spending all his savings on it, his friends were depending on him to do it, the press was watching him. If he didn't manage the swim before the end of August, his dream was over until the following year.

Monday 23rd came, the weather was good enough, Webb decided; he'd leave at midnight that night. But George Toms took a look at the sky – somewhat threatening, he pronounced – and walked down to Dover harbour – too much swell. Better wait another day, he advised. Webb agreed. Another day but no longer, otherwise people would say he'd got cold feet. That night, according to a private note made by one of his friends, he was so overwrought with the tension of waiting that 'he relaxed in his attention to discipline and committed an indiscretion, unusual to him'. He does not reveal the exact nature of this indiscretion but, in the light of Watson's memoirs of London pleasures, the fact that Webb was a sailor and Dover a port, drunkenness and a visit to a prostitute are a reasonable guess.

The morning of Tuesday 24 August broke gloriously. The barometer signalled calm weather, the sky was overcast but not threatening, there was no wind and the sea was 65 degrees and as smooth as green glass. That day Toms had good news; it was his considered opinion that Webb should start that day around one o'clock. It would be about two hours after high tide and Webb could pick up the stream of water speeding into the Straits of Dover from the Atlantic, which would drive him east up the Channel. After that, there would be almost an hour of fairly slack water when he could make good progress. Then, a stream powered by the north sea would sweep him south-west. Toms thought this Z-shaped route would make the best use of the Channel's tides; he reckoned Webb would be able to do it in 14 hours. On the other hand, the captain of the *Castalia* passenger boat, thought to be the man most knowledgeable about Channel conditions in England, said he thought 20 hours was nearer the mark. The truth was, nobody really knew – and Webb was about to find out.

Webb ate a large indigestible breakfast of eggs, bacon and claret and then went down to the harbour. Gathered to accompany him were his cousin, George Ward, his young friend Charles Baker, who'd agreed to swim with him from time to time by way of encouragement, to dive in and rescue him should that be necessary and to cook for the others, Payne who was covering the story for *Land and Water* and the London *Standard* and acting as a referee. The other referee was Henry Wilkinson, who was representing *The Field* and the *Daily News*. Two local reporters, J. B. Jones, editor of the *Dover Express*, and Mr Warman, of the *Dover Chronicle*, were representing the *Daily Telegraph* and *The Times* respectively. The story would be pictured by a Mr Bell, an artist representing the *Illustrated London News* and the *Sporting and Dramatic News*. They all went in one boat. In the lugger were Captain Toms, the lugger's mate, John Dodd, and five crew members, their names Bowles, Jell, Gates, Decent and Stanley. Fifteen people in all, and Webb was the calmest of the lot.

At a quarter to one, the lugger bearing the men, a large piece of bacon, a basket of eggs, a keg of beer and a frying pan, left the harbour, sailing south to the Admiralty Pier. On deck, Webb undressed and oiled himself and then got into a smaller boat and was rowed to the pier. The Admiralty Pier was not designed for pleasure. This long, straight, plain walkway was built from stern Portland stone and concrete; its sole purpose was to provide landing stages for cross-Channel steamers. Still standing, it has none of that air of bloomers and gaslight and kisses that Brighton's Palace Pier evokes, even in its current amusement arcade incarnation. The Admiralty Pier is grim and grey and has hard work written all over it.

However large and encouraging your support team, nothing can change the fact that swimming the Channel is a solo endeavour. It's you who has to do it. You're the only one who strips, shivering in the cold air, who dips a hand into the jar of thick grease and rubs it over your body and who has to get into that uncompromisingly cold water and start swimming.

The momentary hesitation at the end of the pier was Webb's alone, so too was that view into the greenish-black water 10 feet below. The water would be piercingly cold; that was certain. And the waves would slap his face and the salt water sting his eyes and make his tongue sore and so swollen it would feel too large for his mouth. On a clear day, you can see the coast of France from Dover but that day it was hazy and, before he reached the other shore, there would be hard work and an aching body and frozen limbs and a tiredness that goes right through to the bone and perhaps, after all that, failure again. But still he had to dive in.

He waited. For what? He played to the gallery by pointing significantly in the direction of the opposite coast and, perhaps, bought himself just another second. Then, at precisely four minutes to one o'clock, Webb dived into the Channel. The watching crowd gave three cheers but the sounds were blurred because his ears were full of water and soon the noise stopped and it was just him alone, in the silence of the sea.

Payne later recalled that moment, writing with the combination of lyricism and humour that always seemed to surround Captain

Webb: 'as he swam away from the pier, his broad shoulders shooting through the water, and gleaming in the light of the sun, he very much resembled some large seal or huge fish, not merely in smell but in appearance'. Buckland's porpoise oil was clearly pungent.

Just as in a marathon, pacing yourself is essential in a long-distance swim. Pumped up by adrenalin it is easy to start too quickly and leave nothing in reserve for the final stretch. You have to manage somehow to prepare yourself for a long distance but never think of the whole. The idea of swimming the Channel is too big; your brain would say 'Impossible. You can't do it.' So you play tricks with your mind. You tell yourself you just have to worry about the next hour. And when that hour has passed, 'Oh, well, I'll just go on to the next hour.' Or, if that seems too long, then the next half-hour. And when that gets boring, you concentrate on your strokes, put all your focus into making the best arm entry into the water, the longest, strongest pull through. Or you monitor your breathing, taking large breaths, breathing out noisily. Some swimmers play board games in their head or recite the lyrics to songs. Anything will do, anything that distracts your mind from the fact that your body wants to stop.

Webb made a fast start, doing about 25 strokes a minute, but soon slowed down to his more usual 20. And, at first, everything worked smoothly, but then it is always like that at the start of a swim. You feel so powerful and in control, as if you could swim for ever. At a quarter past two, Webb was three miles from the

Admiralty Pier and moving strongly. He was focused inwards, which was how it should be. The sea was smooth and the wind so light the lugger needed to be rowed.

For the men on the boats, it was a monotonous business. Next to them in the water was Webb, in his own private world, moving steadily, hypnotically, through the water. Stroke after stroke, kick after kick, minute after minute, hour after hour. Payne thought it was very dull work. 'To take notes for an hour or two is by no means an unpleasant task, but to drift for twenty hours was rather wearying, especially at times when there was nothing of moment to record,' he wrote. Stroke after stroke, kick after kick, minute after minute, hour after hour.

Next to that smooth, unchanging stroke was the varied business of boat life – marking the map, taking bearings, looking out for boats, chatting and eating. There were long breaks between the swimmer's feeds – and even those were brief. He did not want to stop for too long as not moving would lose him precious body heat. Just a few quick gulps, enough time to say 'All right', and then it was head down and on again. Stroke after stroke, kick after kick, minute after minute. But the observers had time and leisure to look around and take in the sun and enjoy the day. And this day was a great improvement on the nauseous misery of the first attempt; the men on board were enjoying themselves. They called greetings to the mail boats and cheered Webb whenever he looked round at them.

There was time enough for jokes. In the afternoon, just after Webb's first halt – when he drank half a pint of beer – some porpoises appeared. George Toms suggested catching one and boiling it down 'in case the captain's grease fell short', he joked. Payne flourished a small revolver but the porpoise clearly had enough sense to keep out of their way.

There was time enough for one of the crew to borrow the spare boat and row off to examine some objects floating in the distance; he returned triumphantly with an empty barrel. There was time enough to cook a large omelette and enjoy a late lunch, and enough time for messing around so that one of the crew stumbled and overturned a kettle full of hot water and one of the rowers jumped, swearing and complaining. The sea was full of fish, mainly mackerel. At one point they were surrounded by a huge shoal that, darting away from a hungry porpoise, leaped several inches out of the sea and seemed to be flying through the air. They were having a high old time and Webb kept on swimming: stroke after stroke, kick after kick, minute after minute.

There was leisure enough to get angrily patriotic when, at about six o'clock, the French steamer, *Ville de Malaga*, passed close by but not one of the passengers, 'the wretched foreigners', acknowledged their greeting. 'How is it that foreigners cannot cheer?' wondered Payne. 'Yankees shout, Rah! rah! rah! French and Germans etc. Bravo! Bravo! but no one cheers like a true-born Briton.'

There was a little work to be done too. At 6.50 p.m., one of

The *Illustrated London News* shows Webb being handed hot coffee during his Channel swim.

the reporters rowed back to Dover with telegrams from others in the lugger which he duly despatched to their respective newspapers. The news at that point – mid-Channel – was good. Webb told them he was 'going on capitally'. He'd drunk some beer and a little beef tea.

Sunsets are always more spectacular at sea than on land and, when the sun sank shortly after seven o'clock, it was with a trail of red-gold across the water and a rosy light on the sails of distant ships. Swimming in the dark spooks some swimmers; they hate the blackness of the water and having only the light of the boat to guide them, but Webb said that he was 'as right as a trivet and quite warm'. His only complaint was about the amount of seaweed in the water; it trailed slimily about his limbs.

The lugger was frailly lit by gaslight, and through the dimness there glimmered the lights of other vessels and the shore illuminations of still distant Calais. But once night fell entirely, the brightest light came from Webb, who was swimming now in a phosphorescent haze, the watery green glow glinting off his arms and shoulders. Watching his friend, Payne was moved almost to poetry: 'as the bold swimmer struck out each stroke seemed to surround him with a halo of glory, like that shown in the pictures of the early Christian martyrs'. Underneath a star-filled sky, the heavy oars of the lugger splashed showers of diamond-bright water.

On a more practical level, Webb's stroke was still strong with powerful arm movements and a good kick. He was moving high on the water and, watching him, his supporters felt equally buoyant. He smiled when spoken to and some of the men on the boat began to talk confidently about his finishing the swim in less than 14 hours.

At around 9.20, Webb let out a yell: 'I've been stung!' Immediately, there was commotion on the lugger, a confusion of worried voices. 'Lugger ahoy! Let's have that bottle of brandy!' A yellow jellyfish had stung Webb on his shoulder. Called starches by local sailors, these creatures were plentiful in the Channel and Webb dreaded them. Pale yellow in colour, with a thick fringe of long hair-like tentacles, they have a poisonous sting that strikes like a dozen little needles in your skin. He could have seen it as a positive sign, as jellyfish tend to congregate in the middle of the Channel, so a sting meant he was at least half-way across. But perhaps he didn't know that and, in the meantime, there was the pain to deal with. He applied the brandy externally which would have been as good as useless. But he swam on and shouted back that he was 'all right', and that he couldn't feel the sting any more. It was almost certainly the salt water which was healing the smart. It was the first real problem he'd encountered and from then on, worried observers noticed that his stroke, never particularly fast, had slowed even further.

Shortly after 10 o'clock, the moon came up to shine down brightly on the vast expanse of almost motionless water. The lugger lit a red light and everything from its sails to the two small rowing boats and the set face of the swimmer was bathed in a reddish glow. At ten to midnight, they heard the swish-swish of the paddle wheels from the *Maid of Kent*, the Calais mail boat, and then the huge steamer loomed out of the darkness less than 100 yards away. It had come slightly out of its way so its passengers could see Webb. Toms sent up a flare, and from the steamer came cheers and the shrill sound of its whistle. A moment of connection in the dark night, and then the mail boat passed, the cheers died on the wind, the bright lights turned to pinpricks.

And still Webb swam on. He'd been told that, if he could hold out for another four hours, he would swim ashore at Cap Gris Nez.

The moon lit up Calais' white chalk cliffs and the revolving light outside the port seemed very close.

Chapter 6

I'll Stick It as Long as I Can Wag a Toe

You can see the land. It looks really close but it takes forever to get there. You're slower, the tide's strong. You want this swim to be over so badly. You want to finish and for it to be successful. Those last three miles are the worst. Any swimmer will tell you that.

———— *Alison Streeter, 'Queen of the Channel', 1998*

In the water, Webb was struggling. Gloom descended on the whole company. It was nearly three in the morning, Webb was three miles from France and the tide was turning against him. And the observers on the boat were seriously concerned about his physical condition. His stroke was visibly slowing and he seemed drowsy.

The tiredness of a long-distance swimmer is a terrible thing to witness. It's not the sweaty, muscle-throbbing windedness of, say, a 100m sprinter. The exhaustion is total – glazed eyes; weak, sloppy swimming; stroke control gone. The skin turns a weird grey colour

Boy Baker stands stripped and ready to plunge to Webb's aid.

as blood drains away from the surface. The swimmer is in agony. His whole body, even his earlobes, hurts. His shoulders are particularly bad. It is painful to lift his arms. Every stroke has to be executed in the knowledge that it will hurt. Arms feel heavy; it's an effort to lift them out of the water. The mind dissociates and loses control of the body. The brain may be saying 'three kicks' to the leg but the leg is responding with one limp flick. You lose a sense of security about your body and its capabilities. It should be scary but it's not, because your mind is so far gone that it doesn't recognise fear any more. For many swimmers, once the body weakens like this, there is no possible comeback and they slip swiftly into a hallucinatory state.

Webb's friends began to prepare for failure. George Toms warmed up some bricks and Baker stripped off and attached a life belt round his chest, wrapped himself in a coat and sat in the rowing boat, ready to dive in and rescue Webb when the moment came. But the moment never did come. After a slug of brandy and some coffee, Webb rallied, called out 'All right' and went on. He was only managing 16 strokes a minute now but the emergency was over. Baker put his clothes back on.

Dawn came just after four and, shortly after that, the first view of France. Webb took some cod liver oil and continued swimming. The sun may have made things look more cheerful and the sight of land was encouraging, but the tide was thoroughly against him now. The sea was running away from the shore. However hard Webb struck out towards Cap Gris Nez, it slipped away from him. Soon it was out of sight and, instead, he was heading straight for Calais. A nasty east wind was blowing and the sea was getting rougher with every minute; white-crested waves were washing over into the rowing boats. Channel swimmers talk of 'battling the waves' and Webb was battling now. And losing. The waves were beating his face and he was being carried further and further away from his destination. With each passing minute, each stroke, his tiredness increased. He was only swimming 15 strokes a minute and each one was poorly executed. His hands drooped in the water and his fingers splayed open. There was no strength in the stroke. He wasn't swimming so much as surviving.

They did all they could to help him. Baker undressed again and, this time, joined Webb in the water. Calling encouragement, he swam with him across the waves. The men on the lugger and in the rowing boats shouted and cheered. The wind was so fierce that George Toms was struggling to hold the lugger on a straight course. The wind buffeted Webb and his body rolled between the valleys created by the waves. His face looked like that of a corpse but his arms and legs kept moving. 'This sea is killing me by inches,' he cried. And still the land kept slipping away.

He was in agony. So were the observers. Down the years, Warman's report printed in both the *Dover Chronicle* and the *Daily Telegraph* still ring with the tension and torment of the final two hours:

> They were two hours of the greatest anxiety to those who were watching the efforts of the gallant swimmer, and of perfect torture to Webb, whose pale and haggard face told of thorough exhaustion; but his indomitable pluck would not allow him to give up with the prize so near. As he grew weaker the wind and tide became stronger, and still he held on with the most marvellous perseverance, although the seas were breaking over him and obstructing his movements towards land.

Calais at last. An exhausted Webb is helped into the waiting carriage.

At 9.30, Webb had a stroke of luck. The Calais mail boat, the *Maid of Kent*, sent out a rowing boat with eight persons on board. Not only did they add their cheers of encouragement, they rowed on the bad-weather side of Webb which protected him a little from the elements. But it was unlikely that his strength would hold out. He was managing at most 12 strokes a minute, and his legs were dangling uselessly in the water. The lugger had to tack round and round Webb, otherwise the wind would drag it away from him. Toms climbed to the top of the cabin and kept shouting: 'He'll do it,' but Webb was barely keeping afloat.

Surely though the shore seemed nearer? There were the bathing huts on the beach. They were definitely getting nearer. Two hundred yards to go. There was non-stop cheering from the boats. A huge crowd was gathering on the beach. A hundred yards to go. The men on the mail boat were playing 'Rule Britannia'. George Toms was crying, tears pouring down his face. The water felt shallower. Nearly there. The rowers pushed their oars into the water; they were touching the bottom. Nearly there. And, then, finally solid ground. He was there. He had done it.

Exhausted, delirious, his face encrusted with salt, one eye blind from the waves, his body rigid and greasy like a lump of cold wax, Webb stood, stumbled and fell, lifeless, into the waiting arms of his friends.

Chapter 7

$\mathbb{S}$ee the Conquering Hero Comes

I can only say that the moment when I touched
the Calais sands and felt the French soil beneath
my feet is one which I shall never forget, were I
to live for a hundred years.

_____ *Matthew Webb, 1875*

It changes everyone who does it. It reveals
yourself to yourself. There's nothing to do out
there except suffer and think.

_____ *Mike Oram, Channel pilot, 1998*

'What a glorious thing is this triumph of Captain Webb . . .' wrote
the poet Algernon Charles Swinburne a few days after Webb's
crossing. 'What a supremely great man he would have been in Greece.
Man indeed – he would (and should) have been deified on the spot.'

Swinburne was a passionate, perverted swimmer (he considered
bathing in violent waters even more exhilarating than being flogged

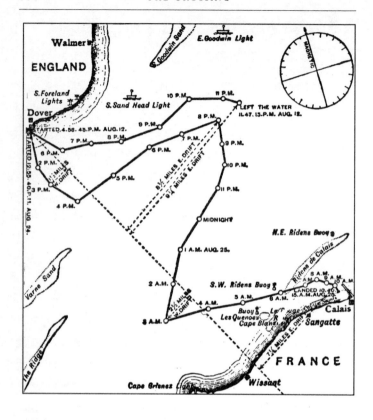

Map from 1875 showing the routes of Webb's two attempts to swim the Channel. The sharp zigzags were caused by the strong tides pushing him off course.

at Eton) and given to hyperbole, but for once he found himself outdone. These days, a Channel crossing rarely makes the news. Then it was more than the news; it was history in the making, a living myth. The references to Ancient Greece came thick and fast. 'Thus was performed a task that might rank with the fabled labours of Hercules – certainly one without parallel in ancient or modern times,' pronounced one newspaper. The satirical magazine *Punch* picked up the classical theme and printed a humorous poem which contained the lines: 'As for Leander, now his fame must sink to nearly zero/For what is he compared with Webb who's in himself a hero?'

The crossing made Webb more than merely famous, it re-cast him in heroic mould. He was seen as a peerless example of English manhood, a role model for the nation's youth. His triumph was Britain's glory, a symbol of the empire's continuing success. 'Men like him are an honour to their country,' wrote the *Telegraph*. 'The triumph at such an achievement as his is one in which the whole nation participates.' The *Standard* went still further: 'This is the stuff of which the hearts of oak of the old days were made, which won Cressy, Trafalgar, Waterloo and Delhi for us.'

He was claimed as evidence of the great Victorian goal of progress, better diet and better living conditions creating better bodies. And a greater knowledge of science had made his swim possible. 'As we advance in knowledge we get to understand better the elements requisite to ensure success,' proclaimed one writer.

'Our power over nature thus becomes more complete; when we try we can accomplish more.' As a national figure, Webb was both reassuring and inspiring, a hero straight from the pages of the past who also celebrated the virtues of progress.

His crossing gave swimming an enormous boost, transforming it almost overnight into one of the most popular participation sports in the country, a position it still holds. Within weeks of his crossing, the nation had taken to the water with gusto. A report in the *New York Times* on 3 October 1875 described how 'Captain Webb has achieved a vast ocean of good by giving an impulse to swimming throughout the country. The London baths are crowded; each village pond and running stream contains youthful worshippers at the shrine of Webb, and even along the banks of the river, regardless of the terrors of the Thames police, swarms of naked urchins ply their limbs, each probably determining that he one day will be another Captain Webb.' Several drunks discussed his swim in taverns and then took headers into the Thames in the spirit of imitation. There was a flurry of 'how to swim' books, three times the number being published between 1875 and 1899 as there had been in the 25 years preceding his crossing.

Swimmers had long complained about the paucity of swimming pools in Britain. Matthew Webb changed all that. Two years after his crossing, the number of swimming clubs had grown to over 200. In 1878, an amendment to the Baths and Wash-houses Act empowered local authorities to build covered swimming baths, stipulating that charges were to be kept low (from as little as 2d to no more than 8d), thus allowing the maximum number of people to use them. Between November and March they were to be covered with a floor and used for lectures, concerts and dances. As a result, the municipal swimming baths became a key part of an area's social life. By the end of the century, local education authorities were paying the entrance fees for schoolchildren, provided that they received swimming lessons. Thanks to Webb, swimming became an essential part of the British child's education, and we can thank him too for the low-priced pools in every town.

All this was still in the future. For the moment, Webb, unaware of the fame which awaited him, as yet unsung and undeified, lay, wrapped in blankets and filled with hot wine, in a deep, sweaty sleep at the Hotel de Paris in Calais, watched over by his cousin George Ward and a local doctor. His skin was hot and damp, his temperature a worrying 101 degrees, his pulse slow and his face flushed deep red with fever. Downstairs in the hotel, a crowd was gathering. The whole of Calais wanted to see this 'half man half fish'. They hung up their hats in the hall, took possession of the salon and gathered beneath Webb's bedroom window. Reporters lounged about, waiting to grab an interview; the English consul in Calais came to pay him a visit. For a day and a night he lay there, his sleep broken only by a short break to eat some soup and fish and once to appear briefly at the window. But at nine o'clock on the morning after his swim, he woke fully, woke to the consciousness of stiffness in his legs and two painful, four-inch red weals on the back of his neck caused by keeping his head well back to avoid the blinding sea spray (they would prevent him from fastening his shirts for a fortnight), woke to a hot bath and a hearty breakfast, woke too to the realisation of his celebrity and perhaps the sense that his life would never be the same again, that he had crossed more than the Channel, that the 21 miles of sea would be for him the passage between private person to public figure, from individual to icon.

His first response to the crowds and the congratulations was to run away. He and Ward chose to behave like ordinary tourists and hired a carriage to take them for a drive in the countryside. On the way, they visited a lace factory where the burly captain was presented, somewhat incongruously, with a dainty lace veil. But that quiet cousinly drive through the flat countryside of the Pas de Calais was only a brief reprieve, the last taste of normality for weeks to come. Webb had to return to face his public.

Back at the hotel, there was an invitation from Captain Pittock of the steamship *Castalia*: would the captain accept the invitation of the Channel Steamship Company and return to Dover in the *Castalia*? Yes, the captain would, but first he had to settle his bill. The landlord had sent in his account, inserting 50 francs for medical attendance. Webb was amused, realising that medical attendance meant simply the local doctor who, uninvited, had felt his pulse and looked at his tongue. Webb laughed and reminded the landlord that he'd arrived in Calais practically nude. He was sorry, he joked, but he hadn't carried a *porte-monnaie* on this journey, but he was so pleased with his swim that he would take care to bring the doctor's fee the next time he swam over.

At one o'clock, Webb and his party said goodbye to the well-wishers in the hotel and set off for the port to find the *Castalia* decked out with flags in his honour. Settled in the salon with Captain Pittock waiting on him, Webb hoped to relax but soon found himself the centre of an excitable little crowd. Word had got out that he was on board and the passengers wanted to see him. Feeling claustrophobic, Webb excused himself and went on deck; the moment he was spotted there, the passengers gave a huge cheer. He sailed into Dover harbour on a wave of applause.

As the boat docked, all he could see was people. The Admiralty Pier he had swum from was packed with noisy, jostling, cheering people, waving handkerchiefs and hats, calling his name. There were flags and bunting everywhere. As he walked up the pier, he was engulfed by bodies pressing towards him, excited faces, eager hands reaching out to shake his. Who were all these people, these strangers who wanted to touch him? In the confusion, his eyes searched out the familiar. There at the gate to the pier stood Captain Toms – it was his victory too – behind him was John Dodd, the mate of the lugger, and with him the rest of the crew – Bowles, Jell, Gates, Decent and Stanley: they were all carrying flags and smiling, their hands held out to greet him. They clasped hands, friends, comrades, sharers in a common endeavour. Beyond the gate and stretching into the town were more people, and his pace slowed down as they crowded round him. Luckily, someone – he never found out who – had brought a carriage. He climbed in, his friends from the lugger followed him. and it was off to the Flying Horse, where a pile of press cuttings, telegrams and invitations awaited him.

He was front-page news; Boyton's exploits were history, the previous hero of the Channel cut down to size, written off as a pushy little New World adventurer with a funny rubber suit and too high an opinion of himself. Webb was a *real* hero, the genuine article. If, in the delirium of exhaustion or the elation of success, Webb had forgotten any detail of his swim, here in the papers, over and over again, was his story in full. Hour by hour, sometimes minute by minute, his long swim was recorded. He was the hero of the story but the story was told by others; any account he gave of himself would always be preceded and, due to his inarticulacy, over-shadowed by those first, hot-off-the-press narratives.

He must have read them with a sense of wonder, perhaps even of disbelief. How did it feel to see himself described as 'probably the best-known and most popular man in the world'? However proud he might have felt of his achievement, it must still have been extraordinary to hear it called 'the greatest feat of swimming yet put on record', and to have your personal triumph transformed into 'a matter of national importance'. Did he recognise himself in the portrait of the 'sturdy, deep-chested young seaman' full of 'British pluck' and 'bulldog spirit'? A few carping voices questioned the value of his swim, wondering how useful it was, the *Liverpool Daily Post* severely misjudging the mood of the moment when it wrote that it was a 'little tired of feats of swimming', and went on to preach that 'People seem to forget that physical strength and endurance are not necessarily admirable things in themselves, but only become so when directed to a moral end.' But the country had gone mad about physical strength and drowned out such criticisms in a torrent of praise and a storm of congratulations. It was as if the whole world wanted a piece of Webb. There were invitations galore, some pleasant, others not so welcome. An invitation to dine that night with the officers of the 24th Regiment at the Citadel Barracks in Dover. Yes definitely. An invitation from the Alexandra Palace Company to exhibit himself on stage. Certainly not. He wasn't interested in anything that smacked of that American circus-owner Phineus T. Barnum and his freak-filled Greatest Show on Earth. A suggestion that he allow his body to be examined by an eminent doctor. Why not? He didn't mind *that* kind of exhibition.

He gave an exclusive interview to the *Daily Telegraph*. Whether he enjoyed it or not we do not know, but the reporter made clear both his expectation: 'An account of his long journey through the water from his own lips would doubtless be most interesting . . .' and his disappointment: 'but the captain is a bad hand at spinning a yarn, and is inclined to be very brief about it'.

'I went,' Webb told the reporter, 'into the water determined either to reach the other side or sink. All I can say is that I kept pegging at it, and it was a terribly hard job towards the end, but I was determined not to give up as long as I had strength to move a limb.' He was reminded about the jellyfish but Webb was in that mellow state of mind that comes after success when the difficulty is over and the pain forgotten. So, yes, the sting brought on faintness but after a drop of brandy it soon went away. And the cod liver oil made him feel ill and he wouldn't take it again. As for the cold in the Channel, why, he felt as warm when he came out as when he went in. There must, he joked, be a double-force pump in his heart. The reporter was right; it wasn't much of an interview. All we learned was that swimming the Channel was very hard work, but he didn't mind the cold and he'd resolved to give up cod liver oil.

If he couldn't speak well, at least he knew how to listen, with an appealing modesty, to all the compliments offered to him. He listened to his health being drunk at the regimental dinner, to extravagant praise by the mayor of Dover: 'In this world there never was such a marvellous exploit as that one which has just been completed by Captain Webb; and I make bold to say that in the future history of the world any such feat will be performed by anybody else.' And to Admiral Hawthorn of the Royal Cinque Ports Yacht Club, expressing his hope that he would see 'this brave, noble and plucky man standing before Her Majesty and the inhabitants of this country to receive that token of approbation that his services demand'.

It didn't matter much, not at this stage at least, that Webb struggled to tell his own story. Any remarks he did make were received ecstatically and for his fans it was enough that they could see him. Sport emphasises the physical over the psychological. Webb's body, what it looked like, the way it performed, how it had suffered in the Channel fascinated the public; a witty, intelligent swimmer would probably have disconcerted them. Better that he was silent and allowed them to fill the vacuum with their own dreams.

There was a tendency to squabble over him. He even quarrelled with Robert Watson. The journalist was annoyed when Webb forgot to write to him after the crossing and wrote reproachfully. According to Watson, Webb 'did not know what the devil he had to thank me for'. Watson smarted over this and in his memoirs muttered dark hints about the dire influence on Webb of 'a certain person who shall be nameless . . . an individual who has always hankered after celebrities when others have, by patience and hard work, created for their prodigies lasting reputation. In the hardy sailor he saw material for the manufacture of very cheaply purchased kudos, and from the day referred to Webb no long bothered himself with those who were the first to secure him a position as a celebrated swimmer.' There was, too, a slight estrangement from Beckwith who also felt that he had put a lot of effort into Webb's swimming career and now felt slighted. Both Watson and Beckwith were being premature; Webb may have been rude but he did not drop them and, within a matter of weeks, the three men were friends again. The nameless person clearly vanished off the scene, but what the quarrel indicated was that very soon after Webb's swim men were prepared to fight over him, to grab at his reputation and use it for their own ends, and that it was easy to persuade him to let himself be so used. Those years spent in the Merchant Service may have taught him the discipline he needed for his Channel crossing, but he was unsophisticated and he lacked a certain judgement, being wholly without the sort of fine antennae that would have told him when he was being exploited.

All the attention seems to have alarmed him. On 28 August, he attempted to escape the crowds and head for his home in Shropshire, but word got out and a mass of people assembled outside the Flying Horse Hotel and then escorted him and Ward to the railway station with the Dover company of the 5th East Kent Rifle Volunteers playing 'See the Conquering Hero Comes'. Once in London, he dashed across town from Charing Cross station to Euston Square. Leaving Dover and London incognito was difficult but preserving any sort of anonymity or even privacy in Shropshire was totally impossible. His home county had prior warning of his arrival and was *en fête*.

At eight o'clock in the evening, Webb's train pulled into the town of Wellington, a few miles from his home. There were flags hanging out of shop windows and the balcony of the refreshment room at the station was crammed with women, their hands full of flowers, ribbons and small banners. Hundreds more people crowded outside, standing on bridges and walls, craning to see Webb. The noise was deafening; the air full of shouts of 'Hurrah for Webb', 'Long live the gallant captain', 'Hurrah for the brave'. It took him half an hour to get out of the station and he had to run a gauntlet of handshaking before he could climb into the carriage sent to collect him by two of his brothers. Even then he didn't get very far because the excited crowd insisted on unharnessing the horses and pulling the carriage themselves. A procession quickly formed. First came the 7th Shropshire Rifles playing 'See the Conquering Hero Comes', followed by men carrying a large Union Jack. Behind them Webb rode in state with his two brothers and George Ward. Two more carriages followed bearing the members of the hastily formed Ironbridge reception committee. Together they moved slowly through the densely packed streets which were lit only by candles held by the men and women who came out to line the route. Beyond them, away in the dark fields, Webb could hear his name being shouted again and again. Beside him ran a particularly enthusiastic admirer, keeping pace with the carriage all the way from Wellington. A laughing Webb leaned down and pulled him, puffing and breathless, to stand on the running board. 'I wanted a good look at your face,' the man said and called for a candle, then gazed long and hard at Webb. 'I shall know thee now from a thousand,' he said. 'What'll you have to drink?' Amused, Webb refused the drink and set his admirer down.

On his way to Coalbrookdale, everywhere he looked there were marvels. The vast mansion of Henry Whitmore shone among the trees, every room lit up in honour of the Channel swimmer. And ahead in the distance was a glow, a fiery illumination that an amazed Webb realised, as the carriage emerged from the trees, was his home town.

Coalbrookdale was ablaze with light. Torches glittered along the banks of the River Severn until it shimmered like a mirror. Bright Chinese lanterns lit up an arch of evergreens decorated on one side with 'Welcome' and on the other 'Hail to British pluck'. Every house shone with lights, everyone on the street carried a torch. There was a sudden moment of silence and stillness as, in the glare from the torches, Webb's face was seen, bewildered and awestruck, then the music of the church bells rang out and the applause, swelling louder and louder, filled the air.

Like a river of torchlight, the procession wound on and on. Past the Rodney Pub, bright with Chinese lanterns and covered with banners and a wreath bearing the words: 'Welcome! Gallant Captain Webb'. At the Tontine Hotel, a five-point star blazed and another brass band struck up. In the overwhelming noise, a few distinctive sounds could still be heard: a popping champagne cork and a small child squirming in his mother's arms squeaking: 'Hurrah for Webb'. The head of the reception committee had to struggle to make himself heard over the cheers, most of his words lost in the noise. 'Dear Captain Webb,' he shouted,

the gratifying task devolves upon me of presenting you
with an address of congratulation and welcome upon
your safe return home after your successful accomplish-
ment of a feat unparalleled and unapproachable, it is
believed, in the annals of the world's history. When your
intended attempt to swim across the English Channel
was first mentioned it was looked upon by many as an
absolute impossibility, but the result has proved that the
same physical strength, pluck and perseverance which
raised England to its proud eminence in former times
still exists, and the inhabitants of Shropshire in general
and Ironbridge in particular, are proud to think that all
these qualities are embodied in one who was born and
reared in their midst. I am only speaking the sentiments
of all who know and feel interested in you when I
venture to express a hope that a youth, which has been
ennobled by such signal acts of bravery, may be followed
by a life devoted to the well-being of your fellow
creatures, and to the praise and glory of Him to whose
mercies alone you are indebted for that wonderful
strength and marvellous power of endurance which have
enabled you to accomplish the tremendous task which
has rendered your name famous throughout the world.
Sincerest congratulations and a hearty welcome.

Then, before Webb had time to absorb these words of praise, it was on past the banners and the Union Jacks and the illuminated stars as outriders in red jackets turned out to escort the swimmer home. His old house was still there but not as he had left it. The orchard was swarming with people, a huge banner declared 'Welcome, welcome indeed' and a band played 'Home Sweet Home'. But his mother was there, smiling her personal welcome, throwing her arms around his neck before leading him indoors and, finally, at long weary last, closing the door on the cheering throng.

The following day was Sunday and not even the presence of Webb in Ironbridge could quite interrupt the peace of a Victorian Sabbath. The Webb family attended a service at Coalbrookdale church and listened to the Reverend Mr Steward preach a sermon on 1st Corinthians ix, 24: 'Know ye not that they which run in a race run all, but one receiveth the prize, so run, that ye may obtain.'

On Monday the celebrations began again with Webb paying a visit to Dawley and Madeley. This time it was a family occasion. His cousin, mother and sister rode with him in a procession consisting of 11 carriages. What Ironbridge had done with lights, Dawley and Madeley were determined to outdo with flowers. The initials M.W. were worked in blossoms and finished off with an anchor. Even the lampposts were decked with evergreens and Webb was showered with bouquets as he made his way to the platform which had been built above the crowds. Everywhere he could read the word Welcome: 'Welcome to the brave'; 'Welcome to Shropshire hero';

Welcome to England's hero'; 'Welcome to thy birthplace, hero'. Webb was in good spirits and inclined to crow over Paul Boyton. He hoped he had done his best, he told the masses. And he supposed if some Yankee came and did the same feat, he would have to attempt to swim the Atlantic. The day ended with an impromptu ball, a huge bonfire and a firework display; at the ball, the ladies changed the words of a song: 'for he is a Dawley man' to 'for he is a darling man'.

And while Webb enjoyed himself as the toast of the county, the money was flooding in. Subscription lists were opened in London, Hull, Birmingham, and the magazine *Land and Water* agreed to print the names of donors. There was another subscription list on the Hull Stock Exchange and the editor of the *Birmingham Daily Post* agreed to accept money on Webb's behalf. A list of donors printed weekly in the magazine *Land and Water* revealed the range of people whose imaginations were touched and wallets opened by Webb's feat. 'A poor old Rabbi' sent a shilling; 'all that I can afford', he wrote. The president of the Mercantile Marine Association of Liverpool contributed £25. 'A few friends at the Grosvenor Arms in Camberwell' gave £1 4s and a little girl known only by the initials A. A. P. sent a shilling. Over 400 members of the Stock Exchange sent £1 each. There was £5 from an MP, Sir Henry W. Peek, and another £5 from Lord Londsborough. A mysterious 'man in green' donated £1 1s, and Messrs Rothschild £20. A few clerks at Messrs Barclay & Co. sent £3 3s. There were informal collections on train journeys and one was started as far away as Malta. J. C. Monsell of

Spitalfied made a contribution, regretting only that he was unable to 'claim the wonderful fellow as an Irishman'. Generous female contributors hid their identities under the all-purpose soubriquet, 'A Lady'.

On 31 August, Webb returned to London on a farewell note of ringing bells and firing cannons. Perhaps he hoped for a rest, assuming that in the vastness of the capital he'd find the peace and quiet granted to individuals by the anonymity of a big city. If so, he was to be disappointed. For the Channel hero anonymity was a thing of the past and privacy was fast disappearing too. A quiet stroll in the City ended in him being recognised and mobbed and having to dive into a hackney cab to make a getaway. When he paid a business visit to the Baltic Exchange to see how his Testimonial Fund was progressing, strangers chased him down Threadneedle Street and insisted on shaking his hand. He brought work to a halt at Lloyd's as the underwriters, brokers and clerks abandoned their work to stand on their desks and cheer him. At the Stock Exchange the crowd clamoured and pressed so hard and so frantically to see him that it became dangerous. Webb darted down a side street and made off in a cab. He produced a thrill of excitement in the attendants at the hammam in Jermyn Street where he went for a sauna and a plunge into the cold bath, and he became the star attraction at the promenade concerts in Covent Garden when the audience turned from the stage to the box that had been provided for him by the theatre owners, Messrs Gatti. The partying was non-stop. He was the guest of the Lord Mayor of London and of the Belgian vice-consul, the toast of a formal dinner in Gravesend, the recipient of a standing ovation at the Royal Cambridge Music Hall, a sensation on the Liverpool Stock Exchange. There were old friends to meet up with again. Payne and Wilkinson, the two referees who'd accompanied him on his journey, invited him to their offices at *The Field* magazine and gave him a celebration lunch and, in early September, he went back to Dover and hosted a dinner for Captain Toms and the crew of the lugger.

He agreed to sit for his portrait, the ambitious idea being to exhibit his likeness throughout Britain and in all the major cities on the Continent. Some shockingly bad poems were written in his honour, one of which began: 'Dear Captain Webb, at lowest ebb,/My spirits were till just now/But your great feat is such a treat/It rubs off all my rust now.' – and a volume of dance music called *The Channel Quadrilles*. He appeared in cartoons and acrostics.

A Captain Webb medal was quickly struck by W. Holmes of Islington, north London and sold to swimming clubs to use as prizes. Holmes called it the 'Captain Webb's Channel Medal'. One side showed Webb alongside the lugger with the cliffs of Dover in the background while the other depicted a wreath of oak and laurel, and it was finished off with a clasp and a red, white and blue ribbon.

Every post brought letters: piles and piles of letters containing congratulations, requests for his autograph, enquiries about his health, invitations from music hall owners and regatta organisers to exhibit himself. Some he answered, others he simply read, noted, tore up and threw away. Otherwise, he pointed out to friends who came to call, the place would be full of letters. He was not a great writer but he was good-humoured about his correspondence, grumbling amiably that he could manage the swimming but that the writing would beat him.

Every day was like his birthday with dozens of presents to open: a pair of 18-carat-gold sleeve links, a set of gold collar studs and a solitaire from friends in Dover including the owner of the Flying Horse Hotel, a silver cup from the 24th Regiment in Dover, a gold watch, a gold cross from the North London Swimming Club, a jewelled tie pin sent by an Indian rajah. He accepted them all with pleasure and gratitude.

One thing he seemed determined to reject – any invitation to become a living exhibit, to appear on stages or at fairs as the latest marvel alongside strongmen or stuntsmen. He was keen to stress that he was a sportsman, not a showman. When a rumour went around that he was to display himself at the Lambeth Baths, he was quick to quash it, writing with dignity to *The Times*:

> Sir, I have received several letters expressing regret that I should have consented to appear at a public swimming entertainment. Will you allow me, by means of your journal, to inform the public, which has been so generous to me, that I have no intention of exhibiting at the

Lambeth Baths on Monday next, but I have simply
consented to be present, and give away the prizes on the
occasion of Professor Beckwith's benefit, and I am sure
none of my friends will think the worse of me for
rendering so small an act of assistance to one who has
been kind to me, and who has recently lost his wife.

He was, however, perfectly willing to display his body to doctors
and seems not to have objected to the resulting report being printed
in the newspapers. It was a medical man – Dr Henry Smith – who
wrote it, but the letters FRCS after his name are at odds with the
slave-auctioneer tone:

I could not fail being struck with the splendid form and
symmetry of his chest, neck, and arms, and I was
somewhat astonished to find him with such good flesh
and so little angularity, as it were, about him. I expected,
after such hard training and such severe exertion, that the
muscles would stand out in relief and be well marked, as
one has seen in prize-fighters and other athletes; but, on
the contrary, there was a considerable development of
other tissue besides that of muscle. On putting him into
various attitudes, however, and making him exert
particular muscles, their fine development and power
were at once noticeable. The triceps especially, as one

THE CHANNEL QUESTION SOLVED.
"COME ALONG, TOBY! WHAT CAPTAIN WEBB HAS DONE, WE CAN DO!!!"

Punch, 4 September 1875.

would expect, is extraordinarily developed. The scapular
muscles and those of the neck are also especially
remarkable. I measured his chest, whilst he was standing
with his arms held above his head, at two points: first on
a level with his nipples, and found that he measured in
that situation forty-one inches and a half; around the
waist, three inches above the umbilicus, the circumference was thirty-five inches and a half. The arm in
circumference, three inches above the elbow, measured
eleven inches and a quarter. The circumference of the

neck on a level with the thyroid cartilage was over fifteen
inches. On examination with the stethoscope I was
astonished at the extraordinary volume of air entering
the lungs at each inspiration. The sounds of the heart
were remarkably clear and healthy.

Despite his expressed wishes, Webb *was* becoming an exhibit. And just as his body was held up by a doctor as an object of wonder, his character – real or imagined – was put on show too, displayed for boyish audiences. Throughout the autumn of 1875, Webb was a popular speaker at boys' schools. He returned, the famous old boy, to his former training ship, the *Conway*, was awarded a pair of silver mounted binoculars engraved with the words 'Presented to Captain Matthew Webb, as an old Conway boy by the present Conway boys, as a token of their admiration of his great pluck and endurance in the unparalleled feat of swimming across the Channel. September 1875', and was held up to the boys as a perfect role model who was 'motivated by the patriotic idea that an Englishman would do more than an American had done', and whose 'marvellous performances' had 'a manly humility'. At Old Hall School in Shropshire, the headmaster called him a 'noble example', whose determination to attempt the Channel after his failed first attempt showed young boys how you should always try again, and that it was a 'noble resolution' that 'made him a great man'.

Over and over again Webb's presence was used as a springboard for nationalistic bragging. To his credit, he never made such claims himself, never attempted to elevate his individual success into anything bigger. Whatever he thought in his heart, whatever praise he whispered to himself in the dark hours of the night, on the surface he was never conceited. In fact, his friend Buckland at *Land and Water* thought he didn't puff himself up enough. 'There is very little risk of his being spoilt by the adulations of the crowd,' read one of his editorials. 'His fault, if anything, lies the other way; he is too modest.' In his speeches Webb never offered more than a sort of 'it's dogged as does it' explanation for his success in swimming the Channel, and his only declared wish was to see the sport of swimming made more popular, more cheap baths built and fewer lives lost at sea. He was no Boyton, lacking altogether the American's sense of showmanship and his gift of the gab. A speech Webb made to the working men of Dover at a dinner in his honour was typical of the man. In reply to a particularly grandiloquent address in which he was introduced as the man who 'had proved for one thing that the physical condition of Englishmen had not degenerated; that the Englishman of the present day was in no degree inferior to his forefather', he simply said:

> I hope what I have done in the way of swimming is not altogether useless, although really it may not be of much value. I hope it will encourage swimming amongst our people more than it is at present encouraged. I think it is a great shame for a lot of people who live by the sea not

to be able to swim and to be drowned because they can't
swim a yard . . . I think everyone should learn to swim
when they are young, as it is very difficult to learn when
you are grown-up; if what I have done will tend to give
encouragement to swimming, I shall have done a great
deal.

The tentativeness of his wishes, the repetition of the words 'I hope',
the use of 'if', the self-effacing negatives all show a man either un-
naturally unassuming or a man unsure of what he has achieved and
what it will mean to him. He did show himself, on occasions, to be
annoyed by the lack of recognition from royalty. Unlike Boyton, Webb
received no congratulatory telegram from the Queen, a fact he
referred to from time to time. It's also possible that he was embarrassed by the rugged role he seemed to have been cast in. His elder
brother Thomas with, it is fair to assume, Webb's approval, sent one
of Webb's sketches to the *Graphic* newspaper, with the following
letter:

Though Captain Webb is pretty well known at present,
and all his acts and deeds from his cradle upwards, I
believe it is not known to any, except his personal
friends, that he is an admirer of fine art, and a fair judge
of what a picture should be. Though he never had a lesson
in drawing, some of his water-colour sketches are

Webb as he appeared in *Vanity Fair*, 9 October 1875.

extremely good. Thinking that perhaps anything from his hand would be interesting at present, I have sent you a little sketch of his from nature, entitled 'Small Game' – a cock-sparrow and a piefinch, shot by himself, and drawn I think you will say very faithfully and well. Though I am sorry to say he has not used his pencil much of late, I think this little picture of his will prove that he is not merely the 'apostle of brute strength' some would represent him.

Was Webb already chafing against the restrictions his heroic status created?

In late September, Randall's book, *Captain Webb, The Intrepid Champion Channel Swimmer*, was published, reinforcing the image of the plucky, modest young Englishman, inspired by Christian virtues and a love of his country. The book's subtitle, 'containing original particulars of his life supplied by his friends', made its depiction of Webb seem true to life. Webb's own book, *The Art of Swimming*, 111 pages, priced 2s 6d, with a blue cover and gold writing and a picture of Webb, the Stanhope medal on his chest, looking off to the right, also came out in the autumn. On the front it said: 'Edited by A. G. Payne' in small letters, but he was in fact the real author. We have no idea how much input Webb had into the book; it's possible he just lent his name to it and let his ghost writer do all the work, but he always stood by it, calling it 'one of the best' accounts of his swim. It is a curious little hybrid of a book. It begins with an autobiographical section, supposedly written by Webb, which takes the reader swiftly through his career. This is interspersed with various snippets of advice for boys, most of which are borrowed from *Tom Brown's Schooldays* or Polonius in *Hamlet*. It is reasonable to assume that these literary allusions were Payne's work; Webb may have read *Tom's Brown Schooldays* but it's unlikely that lessons on the *Conway* gave him an intimate knowledge of Shakespeare. There is plenty of advice for wholesome manly living, for example: 'For young lads, therefore, I would recommend the following simple directions. Go to bed early, say between ten and eleven, and get up between five and six, do not smoke, and if you have been accustomed to drink beer, one glass with your dinner and one with your supper will be more than sufficient.'

The book also contains Webb's account of his Channel crossing, Payne's recollections of his first failed attempt and some tips on swimming techniques. In Payne's hands, Webb becomes a swimming evangelist, saying the following words: 'I hope the time will, before long, come when no boy can say: "I cannot swim", without the same blush of shame with which an ordinary English schoolboy would say "I cannot play cricket" or "I cannot catch a ball" or "I dare not fight".' The book's emphasis on boys' education and its endorsement of muscular Christianity point to Payne, the athletic Cambridge graduate, not Webb, the merchant seaman. But there is something convincingly Webb about the statement: 'If you firmly make up your mind that you will never tell a lie, not only to your master, but to your schoolfellows, I will undertake to say that in less than six months, you will be thoroughly respected by all around you.'

The swimmer Harry Parker contributed a chapter which extended the book into the realms of philanthropy. Parker taught at the City of London Baths and he wrote a plea for the building of more pools to ease the health and hygiene problems of the urban poor.

> Many attempts have been and are being made to raise the
> lowest strata of the London poor to a higher level.
> Perhaps none of these attempts are more worthy of
> notice than the efforts to instil into their minds a love of
> cleanliness. Certain, however, is it that the London
> swimming baths are the means of bringing water in
> contact with hundreds of thousands of lads who would
> otherwise swell the ranks of the great unwashed.

It sits oddly in a book about Webb, and you have the sense of a man being hijacked to help someone else's cause. Perhaps life in London and friendship with men like Payne had persuaded Webb of the social benefits of swimming and swimming pools, perhaps he believed every word of the book which bore his name, but the fact remained that they were not his words. At this point in his life there were many people willing to speak for him and he seemed to disappear under the weight of his fame. The real Webb was wrapped in a victory toga and smothered.

Another book published that year, *The Channel Feats of Captain Webb and Captain Boyton with Memoir of Each*, probably irritated him as he never got over his dislike of Boyton and resented being compared with him.

In the middle of the celebrations, Boyton quietly slipped away to Germany. Too smart a man not to know when he was beaten, and no doubt sick of hearing how Webb had eclipsed him, he took up an engagement at Baden Baden. His plans were simple: Merriman's Patent Waterproof Life-Saving Apparatus and his 'Amusing, Clean and Interesting Show' would make his fortune.

But what about Webb? What did he want to be? The end of 1875 saw him, in Payne's words, 'in an atmosphere of conquering hero, champagne and kindness'. But although swimming had found its champion and England a hero, Matthew Webb still had to look for a job.

Chapter 8

What Next?

Can there be any position more awful than that of a man who has been a nine days' wonder on the morning of the tenth day? He rises and peeps through the blind, the crowd held in check by the policeman on special duty is no longer at his door. He tears open the paper, and, agony! there is nothing about him, either on the front page or on the back one, there is only a short paragraph which, to the experienced eye, is the forerunner of fame for the next coming man. Was it, after all, but a long dream – a dream of sudden elevation to elective kingship, and a levee at which you received all the world? What strange figures come and go in an instant in that phantasmagoria of memory! The former leader of society, gracious and amiable, who abdicated in your favour with such an air of perfect content; the pretty women,

who condescended to ask you for particulars . . .
Only for nine days! There is the tragedy of it.
_____ The Times, *25 September 1875*

St James's Hall in Regent Street was poorly lit and the few people who had bothered to turn up seemed listless and bored, their voices hushed, their manner funereal. No doubt Robert Watson could think of a hundred better ways to spend a Saturday night but he was there, good friend that he was, to witness Webb's first public appearance as a lecturer. Watson had advised him against it, concerned that it would be the first step on the road to being a full-time showman, but the drab appearance of the hall and the empty seats convinced him that the swimmer was also wasting his time. 'It required,' he thought, 'but a most indifferent knowledge of the world to at once come to the conclusion that the affair would be a failure as a speculation long before proceedings commenced.' It was only 10 months after Webb's great Channel swim and he had already ceased to be a crowd-puller. There was an embarrassingly long delay to wait for a crowd that never materialised and then Webb, smarter than usual in evening dress, appeared. The theme of his speech was 'his life and exploits', and his small group of fans listened with polite attention as he talked his way through his career. The problem was that it was all too well known to be interesting. Learned to swim when he was seven, joined the *Conway* aged 12, travelled the world, decided to swim the Channel, failed the first time, tried again, took a little beef tea, coffee and brandy by way of refreshment, no mechanical aids like that Boyton fellow, just good honest British determination, hoped other people would be inspired by his example to take up swimming.

The contrast with his public appearances shortly after the crossing was painfully obvious. Gone were the hordes of people, gone too the banners, the flowers, the illuminated stars, the enthusiastic cries of welcome. Webb had had his hour in the sun and now his light was fading.

Financially, he was only just comfortable. In March, the Webb Testimonial Fund had been wound down; contributions had reached £2,424 4s 11d. Some of it he gave to his father whose ill health had restricted his practice, and he invested nearly £2,000 which brought him an income of £89 a year, less than that of a lower-middle-class clerk. It wasn't nearly enough. Webb had learned to enjoy himself and he was still famous enough to be lionised by society hostesses and sporting peers. Since his Channel swim, he'd become a member of the Junior Garrick Club, joined the Masons and, according to Robert Watson, 'went the pace like a veritable Corinthian. Life in London was enjoyed to its fullest extent.' He was still friends with Frederick Beckwith, giving away prizes at the promoter's events and publicly acknowledging his debt to the man, but the dismal turn-out at St James's Hall must have convinced him that he was last season's news.

He began to cast around for something to do. He thought of

buying a steam tug in Liverpool and going into business and he considered becoming a swimming teacher, but both these options must have seemed too quiet and private after his noisy success. In July, he proposed, how seriously it is hard to say, attempting to swim from Scotland to Ireland, a 19-mile stretch of unpredictable water where the temperature does not rise above 58 degrees. It never happened.

In August, Webb was up against a different sort of challenge: how to put a brave face on the fact that another man was about to try to swim the Channel. His name was Frederick Cavill and he was a 37-year-old former sailor and winner of no fewer than three Royal Humane Society medals for life-saving. He'd served an apprentice-ship on Queen Victoria's yacht *Fairy* where, it was rumoured, he'd acted as unofficial whipping boy for the transgressions of young Prince Albert (later King Edward VII). He was a strong swimmer, at one time the fastest man in England over 500 yards. Formerly a coach in Brighton, he was now the owner of the Kensington Swimming Baths, where he continued his connection with royalty by coaching one of the Queen's cousins, Princess Mary, Duchess of Teck, to swim. Cavill was to play a key role in the development of swimming in Australia after emigrating there in 1878 and he was one of the first people to use and teach the stroke that is now called front crawl. But in 1876, he was just another London swimming-club owner, physically strong but past his best. A forceful personality with a blunt, outspoken manner, he was quarrelsome and made enemies easily; Robert Watson was a lifelong adversary, the journalist always complaining that Cavill never paid for his adverts in *Swimming Notes*. Although his swimming had always been noted for speed rather than stamina, when he announced his interest in swimming the Channel, he was taken seriously and Webb wouldn't have been human if he had liked it. And Cavill copied freely from Webb, using porpoise oil and even hiring George Toms, his crew and his lugger to accompany him across. Webb felt such a personal interest in the outcome that he joined the boat accompanying Cavill; his young friend Boy Baker and Payne went along too.

Webb needn't have worried; it was a disaster. Poor Cavill made a speedy start but was forced to slow down after swimming through shoals of slimy jellyfish whose stings made him feel sick. To make matters worse, his supporting team fed him far too much whisky. But it was a brave attempt; Cavill swam from three in the morning until one o'clock the following afternoon, when it was clear that not only had he no chance of reaching the other side but his life was in danger. His stroke was weak and his mind so disorientated that he could no longer swim in a straight line by the time one of his friends plunged in and pulled him out. His pulse was alarmingly weak and he had no idea where he was. He was probably drunk, having taken at least half a pint of whisky.

Webb wrote about the event in *Land and Water*. Perhaps he was so relieved that his position as Channel champion was untouched that he forgot to be generous. He criticised Cavill's swimming:

'Cavill uses the side-stroke, and seems to be but an indifferent breast-swimmer, but although the side-stroke is faster, I still maintain that for long distances and rough water, and everything but speed, the old-fashioned breast-stroke is best of all'; his choice of swimwear: 'It was bad policy to wear the jersey, as such a thing must hold a large quantity of water, and also impede the action of the limbs'; and Cavill's physical condition: 'grampus-like breathing . . . making very slow progress . . . dreadfully fagged . . . looked very distressed . . . apparent that he could not get across . . . delirious'. But the remark that most enraged Cavill was Webb's suggestion that he'd only made it half-way across, and he responded smartly, insisting that the pilot's opinion was that he'd gone 14 miles as the crow flies and was past mid-Channel. 'Captain Webb told me he had no means of judging the distance, and that he guessed I was about mid-Channel.' Having knocked Webb's judgement, he insinuated that Webb's swim had been easier: 'Unfortunately for me, I had a nasty "popping" sea which affects a side-stroke swimmer more than a breast-stroke one.'

Cavill now seemed consumed by the desire to beat Webb at the Channel. In July 1877, he gave it another shot, this time making the attempt from Cap Gris Nez to Dover. Webb stayed away but his horror and dismay can easily be imagined when, on 25 August, Cavill declared himself successful and with a crossing time faster than Webb's by nearly 10 hours. Doubts were immediately raised to be first silenced by a signed report from men who'd observed the swim and then raised again when one of the witnesses, a Mr Gammon, was found not to exist. Gradually the complete story emerged. Once again Cavill had been pulled from the water, this time ice-cold and barely breathing. He never admitted his failure or his lie, always insisting that he was the second man to swim the Channel and continuing to provoke Webb whenever he could. In September, he challenged Webb to a race across the Channel. 'I have heard the genuineness of Webb's swim questioned,' he wrote tauntingly. 'Therefore I hope he will accept my challenge and again swim the Channel in company with me, so as to set aside all doubts, and also test our relative merits.' Webb declined. 'I have invariably declined to take any notice of such challenges,' he said. 'Not because I wished to retire altogether as a public swimmer, but because I believe that my engaging in any such matches would result in no good to me were I to win, and in considerable injury were I to lose.'

At the end of the 1876 swimming season, Frederick Beckwith moved into the King's Head public house in Lambeth and threw a party to celebrate. It was the perfect opportunity for Webb to reflect on the past year. It was all very well to stand on his dignity with Cavill but he could hardly pretend that 1876 had been profitably spent; he had simply frittered away his time. The Beckwiths had been very busy, taking their shows all over the country; J. B. Johnson had returned from a swimming tour of the United States and was swimming well; the competition between young Willie Beckwith and Harry Parker had intensified – and all Webb had done was quarrel with Cavill.

The following year, a combination of financial pressures, boredom and a desire to retain his position of champion swimmer forced him out of his semi-retirement and he staked £100 at odds of 20 to one that he could swim the Thames from Gravesend to Woolwich. He looked good, the public's waning interest in him had slowed down his social life and his health was better. On 13 July, in just under 10 hours he broke another record. The 40 miles he covered were the longest freshwater swim on record. But, as anyone who knew the river would realise, it was easier than it sounded because Webb was always swimming with the tide. His next project – from Woolwich to Gravesend and back again – floundered when strong winds and a rough river forced him out of the water after nine hours. He'd managed to achieve some publicity for his ventures by diligently calling attention to them in letters to *The Times*, but he must have been aware that so far he'd failed to deliver another sensation. Meanwhile, Beckwith had livened up the season by introducing 'the original man-fish', a certain Mr T. Atwood, who did water gymnastics in a glass tank.

Disappointment drove Webb further and further under Beckwith's influence. The promoter had been struck with the popularity of a new sort of endurance test. Long feats of walking, swimming and cycling – sometimes for days at a time – had all recently taken place in England and America. The biggest sensation had been Edward Weston, an American who came to Britain and stunned everyone by walking 450 miles in a week. Under the pretence of sporting excellence and even scientific interest, these extreme marathons pushed men far beyond the point of exhaustion. They made fascinating though grisly viewing, but were horribly cruel to the participants. Webb's friend Frank Buckland, although a lover of the unusual, hated them and used *Land and Water* to protest forcefully against them. 'There is no knowing what may still be in store for us,' he wrote angrily. 'Perhaps a forty days' fasting match at the Agricultural Hall. No doubt a row of ghastly skeletons on the verge of dissolution would draw the British public.' Beckwith, on the other hand, noted the public's interest in Weston and asked himself, why not a swimming marathon? He began the 1879 swimming season by announcing a six-day swimming contest to be held at Lambeth Baths. Whoever swam the furthest distance in the six-day period would be the winner. He advertised the event with his usual flair, billing it as the 'long-distance championship of the world' and offering generous prizes: £70 for the winner, £15 for second place, and £10 and £5 for third and fourth respectively. And to attract the maximum number of competitors, anyone travelling over 50 miles had their railway fare paid. The contestants were given star billing: Webb was the 'Channel hero'; Beckwith's son Willie, 'the London champion'; Fearn, 'amateur champion'; while Taylor from Rochdale and Rowbottom from Manchester were 'local champions'.

On day one, it looked as if Beckwith had hit on a winner. The takings on the gate were good, the crowd large and with enough members of the aristocracy to make it feel like a society event. Robert Watson remembered the Westminster Road being lined with carriages and footmen with powdered hair and the Lambeth Baths thronged with 'Haughty peers, newly fledged men about town with handsome fortunes, generals, colonels, captains, majors, political magnates, literary geniuses, millionaires, cotton lords, the money-lending spider with his unsophisticated fly, and the well-dressed thief being present in abundance, eager to witness, for the first time, the Channel hero exhibit the stroke, as they termed it, by which he managed to attain such an exalted position.'

There would be a maximum of 14 hours' swimming a day, starting at nine in the morning and finishing at 11 o'clock at night. Like all Beckwith's events, it was well organised. The pool was divided into lanes by lengths of string to ensure that the swimmers didn't collide, and there were a number of timekeepers and a referee to make sure they didn't miss any laps. The water was a pleasant 71 degrees and the spring sunshine sparkled through the glass roof on to the water. Shortly after nine o'clock, Frederick Beckwith started off the competitors. The first hour saw fast Willie Beckwith the first to complete a mile with Taylor second, Fearn third, Rowbottom fourth and a slow and steady Webb last. Rowbottom stayed in for only three quarters of an hour before disappearing on a tour of the gin palaces along the Westminster Road, and a leisurely breakfast by Fearn changed the picture entirely. Webb was now in third place, and by plugging steadily away managed to overtake Taylor, who was faster but needed more breaks. At the end of the first day, the scoreboard next to the dressing rooms read: Beckwith 17 miles 12 lengths, Webb 17 miles 8 lengths, Fearn 15 miles 4 lengths, Taylor 13 miles, Rowbottom 7 miles 24 lengths.

Webb was the only one of the competitors to start on time the next day. Most of the others, when they appeared, seemed to be flagging already. Beckwith was much slower, complaining of cold and a swollen knee, and Rowbottom and Taylor stopped frequently for breaks. But Fearn still looked good and finished the day second to Webb. By day three, it was clear that only Webb, Beckwith and Fearn were still in the competition. Rowbottom gave up entirely and never got back in the water and Taylor managed only just over two miles. By Thursday, even Webb's formidable stamina began to give way, he ached all over and his right eye was inflamed and had to be bandaged; he looked so exhausted that some onlookers seeing him for the first time refused to believe he was the tough sailor who'd swum the Channel. Friday was the worst day: at one point it seemed that all the competitors were too exhausted to appear in the water and Beckwith had to improvise by sending his daughter Agnes in to perform some of her ornamental swimming. On Saturday Beckwith doubled the entrance fee but there was still a reasonably sized crowd to watch the finish. By 11 o'clock that evening, the scores were: Webb 74 miles, Fearn 62 miles 30 lengths,

Beckwith 42 miles 12 lengths, Taylor 26 miles 8 lengths. For Webb there were bouquets and cheering and the £70 prize money was very welcome, but it couldn't really be called a total success. There were too many people who thought, like Robert Watson, that London had better entertainment on offer than 'watching a very slow swimmer methodically traverse length after length with monotonous regularity'. Webb must have been aware that the event hadn't helped his reputation at all.

Beckwith soon laid on another marathon – a two-day swimming competition – but Webb did not take part; he was busy with his new project, organising a trip to the United States. The failed Channel swimmer, Johnson, had been a huge success in the States, returning with reports of the Americans' interest in swimming and the excellent opportunities for making money. Webb must have reasoned that the successful Channel swimmer would do even better. Cavill had recently gone there and word had it that Boyton, too, was back in his home country, paddling in his suit and boasting about what he'd achieved in England.

On 9 July, in company with the Beckwiths, Webb gave a farewell exhibition of swimming at North Woolwich Gardens, and the following day he travelled to Liverpool to catch the steamer to New York. His hopes were high, but the irritating Cavill was already there and unwilling to let Webb's arrival go without provocation. As soon as he set foot in America, Webb saw Cavill's cocky challenge, published in the *New York Herald*:

F. Cavill, the champion long-distance swimmer of the
World, by virtue of having swum from France to England
in twelve hours, that being half the time that Captain Webb
or Boyton took or by my swim of 21 miles in the Thames,
July 9 1876, in less than six hours, that being the longest-
distance swim on record, do hereby challenge Captain
Webb to test our relative merits in a six days' swimming
match, and settle the question of supremacy on the terms
that he has been doing in England during my absence, viz.;
to swim for 14 hours a day in bathing costume in the sea
off Coney Island, or any place that may offer the greatest
inducements for the same to be carried out.

Every word was calculated to annoy and Cavill was only being
mischievous because he left New York the day the challenge
appeared. But it was a nasty welcome and the first hint that Webb
was not going to have things his own way in the United States.

America must have startled Webb. If his friends in England were
worried about the flashiness of a public lecture or the exploitation
involved in a six-day swimming contest, what would they have made
of the swimming scene in America where competitions were
sponsored by hotels and resorts organisers without reference to the
demands of the sport or the comfort of the competitors? The first
event arranged for him by his new manager, a Captain Henry
Hartley, must have brought the difference between the two

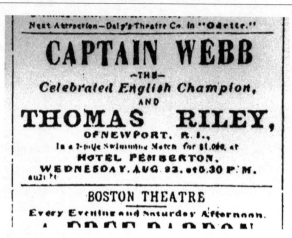

Seaside entertainment: Webb performs at a hotel in America.

countries home to him. He was to swim from Sandy Hook to Manhattan Beach, a 10-mile stretch of the Atlantic at the northern tip of the New Jersey coastline. The Manhattan Beach Company would provide the judges and wager $1,000, the only condition being that Webb would enter the harbour of Manhattan Beach between five and six o'clock in the evening when the greatest number of people would be able to see him. Basically, Webb was being hired to complement the rifle range and 10-cent curiosity museums of this downmarket resort, just another freak at the seaside, another seasonal marvel for the day-trippers from New York to gawp at while enjoying their beer, sausages and clam chowder on the boardwalk.

There were other things to get used to. Unlike in Britain, the press was unfavourable. The *New York Times*, while acknowledging that the swim, if accomplished, would be 'one of the biggest feats of the kind ever performed', was still highly critical: 'First we had Paul Boyton, an American, and now we must put up with an Englishman named Matthew Webb, sometimes called by boastful Britons 'the hero of the Channel'. We can see no possible good in these long-distance swims and the performers are quite apt to overtask themselves in attempting them . . . If one wants to go from Long Beach to Coney one had better take the steamer . . .'

Even more disorientating was the fact that he didn't really know the 13 men – a mixture of hoteliers, reporters and sportsmen – who would be accompanying him on his swim. In long-distance swimming, the relationship between swimmer, pilot and crew is all-important. Only one person actually gets in the water but the project is a team effort; the swimmer needs the support and encouragement, not to mention the food and drink, provided by the crew. This time, the accompanying steam launch *Priscilla* was not being handled by his old friend Captain Toms and it arrived at Sandy Hook annoyingly late. He wouldn't have felt secure with the pilot, who was nervous and inexperienced and openly predicted that the whole thing would be a disaster. There was no Boy Baker around to share his pound and a half of beefsteak at breakfast, and no Beckwith to watch him grease himself with Vaseline and dress in his blue tights and blue jockey cap. It was a lonely figure who stood in the bow of the boat as it steamed into Sandy Hook. At 9.22 on 13 August, he turned his back on its holiday cottages and fishermen's nets, waded out from the shore and began to swim with the ebbing tide.

One thing he could count on was his swimming. He was lighter than usual, weighing in at just under 14 stone, and his breast stroke was honed to a sleek perfection, 29 strokes to the minute, faster than when he swam the Channel, arms cutting widely through the water, his body a long straight line between strokes, his legs moving cleanly, with machine-like regularity.

It was the best kind of swimming, moving without effort; the only problem were his eyes that were becoming bloodshot. He swam through jellyfish (mercifully the non-stinging kind) and shoals of strange fish, moss bunkers that jumped over and around him. Flocks of birds and a pair of butterflies hovered about his head. Webb swam on and on, seemingly tireless. He was 'all right', he replied when anyone from the boat called to him, 'not at all tired', and when the representative of the Manhattan Beach Company was sick overboard, he joked, 'that will satisfy the sharks I guess', and laughed as loudly as the men on board.

He called greetings to the pilots of the tugs whose crews stared open-mouthed at him and gazed back at the holidaymakers on board the fancy yachts. One, the *Nelly*, didn't go away, hovering near the swimmer till he was forced to keep turning his head to look at her. Finally, when everyone was watching the boat, a white figure ran to the edge of the *Nelly* and threw himself in, swimming swiftly towards Webb. It was a man wearing a white handkerchief tied about his head and Webb, surprised, took one look at him and blurted out: 'I thought you were bald-headed.' It was Ernest Von Schoening, an impressive young swimmer from Brooklyn. Schoening explained that he had intended to start with Webb but he had got the time wrong. For the next three hours he swam beside Webb, occasionally diving underwater and displaying a variety of strokes. If Webb was irritated at having some of his thunder stolen, he didn't show it, just kept on swimming.

The *Priscilla* began to find herself in difficulties, tossed about by the same southerly wind that was pushing Webb on to his goal. It had been increasing steadily until by midday it was blowing about 20 miles an hour and the men on board were joking nervously about whether it was better to join Webb in the water now or wait to be thrown out.

At half past one, Webb paused to eat some beef and drink some lager, his favourite old ale having been forgotten. Schoening was still with him and the two men then made for Manhattan Beach. About a mile from the shore they stopped and Schoening reboarded his yacht. It was two o'clock and Webb had to spend three hours in the water in order to fulfil his contract. The tide and the wind were against him, both pushing him in the direction of the beach. There was something mad about having a long, tiring struggle to stay *away* from his destination. The sea hurled Webb about till he bobbed like a cork on the surface of the water, swept up to the top of the huge white-crested waves, dashed down to the hollows.

With every minute the weakness of the *Priscilla* was becoming more apparent. She was too small and too open for such a rough sea and her pilot was both incompetent and cowardly. He flatly refused to stay and declared that he would head immediately for shore. An angry Webb suggested that he and the equally mutinous engineer be thrown overboard. Only when the waves were washing over the sides of the boat and the pilot seemed to have lost his head entirely was an emergency consultation called. It was clear that the *Priscilla* needed better handling if she was to remain afloat. Henry Hartley and a Major Easton decided to stay with Webb, transferring to a small boat while the *Priscilla* headed for shore as quickly as possible. The men in the small boat had the best of it. The pilot was now so terrified that he hardly knew what he was doing and would have simply rammed the boat on to the beach if he hadn't been forcibly restrained by some of the other men. Finally they made it, drenched and miserable and only just before Webb.

Tired but triumphant, Webb strode out of the sea and made his way to the Manhattan Beach Hotel where he was cheered to the echo and surrounded by ladies waving handkerchiefs and Union Jacks. It was a little, just a little, like the reception after his Channel swim, but he seemed too tired to enjoy it because all he did was take a bath, eat a steak supper and return that evening to New York and his bed. He didn't even stay to meet Captain Paul Boyton, who had just arrived at Manhattan Beach.

That meeting – the first face-to-face one between the two rivals – took place four days later on 17 August at the Fifth Avenue Hotel where they both deposited $1,000 and declared themselves ready to race. It is impossible that they liked each other. Webb despised Boyton's apparatus and Boyton knew that his Channel feat was less impressive than Webb's. They said nothing about their hostility and let Henry Hartley do the talking. It would be a spirited race, he told the press conference the following day. The date was to be 22 August, the starting time two o'clock in the morning, the place the main beach in Newport, a fashionable resort popular with New Yorkers. Two white buoys would be placed in the water, half a mile apart. Webb, wearing only his bathing tights, would swim 20 times around the buoys and Boyton, in his life-saving suit, would paddle 25 times. The last lap would be made from the nearest buoy to the shore, which was a mile away.

Everything was arranged for the convenience of the public. People on shore could see the entire race and the finish would be right in front of them. As well as the $1,000 staked by each of the two men, James Garden Bennett, owner of the casino at Newport, put up a further $1,000. The referee would be Herman Oelrich, one of the casino's shareholders. Formal articles of agreement had been signed, covering everything from clothing to be worn, to how food should be handed to the contestants, to the penalties for touching each other in the water. Webb, Hartley added, was in fine form and had no doubt that he would win the match. Boyton spoke to the press separately, allowing himself to be interviewed in the sea off Manhattan Beach by a reporter from the *New York Herald*.

Just before two o'clock on the morning of 22 August, Captain Hartley woke Webb and took him to the beach. There were already more than 100 people there. Some had been there for an hour and were strolling about in the dark, waiting for the race to begin. Webb got himself ready quickly, ate his breakfast, boarded the boat which was to take him out to the buoy, oiled his body and put on his swimming tights. The southerly wind was cold against his skin and the sea was dark and rough. But as soon as he heard his name called by the referee, Herman Oelrich, he stood up and prepared to plunge in.

'Where is Captain Boyton?' asked Oelrich.

Holding a lantern but still looking for all the world like a porpoise, Boyton loomed out of the dark sea. 'Here I am, sir,' he called and paddled to where Webb stood. 'Well, Captain Webb,' he said, putting out his hand. 'There are only two of us and one has to win. If I lose I shan't think more of you, and if I win I shan't think less of you than I do. Which is it going to be?' Webb replied: 'If you will call around about six o'clock tonight I will tell you.'

And then they were off, heading for the outer buoy where a lantern danced and bobbed on the waves. Five minutes later, the light was reflected on Boyton's paddle as he turned round the buoy.

Two minutes later, Webb made the turn. He continued to move slower than Boyton but seemed unworried. At one point he ostentatiously displayed his lack of concern by calling for a cigar and smoking it as he floated on the water.

Dawn broke at five and the sun rose on new arrivals, come to see the fun. Groups of men lolled about on the beach and on the grass behind it, their huge lunch baskets showing that they intended to make a day of it. The scoreboard on the beach showed that Boyton was still in the lead, Webb trailing by nearly a mile, but anyone close to them would have seen that the American was suffering more. Every so often he laid his paddles down on the water and flexed his fingers and arms as if he had cramp.

By seven, carriages were appearing on the beach drive and women had come to join the groups of men. Boyton completed his sixth mile and Webb was already behind the time that the five-mile handicap would allow. Neither man was in good condition, and they were struggling in the high sea, steering an erratic course between the two buoys. Webb had covered his eyes with a green veil. By nine, the beach had come alive. There were people everywhere, along the sand and up the hill, the roads were filled with carriages. Support went in Webb's direction; there was a feeling that he deserved to win because he swam unaided while Boyton had a life-preserver – but Boyton had gone nine miles and Webb only seven.

And at just after 10, it was all over. Webb could be seen in the stern of his boat, wrapped tightly in blankets. Speculation ran through the watching crowd. He must be ill. Perhaps he'd been doing too much, swimming too hard. Or maybe he wasn't acclimatised to the sea. News quickly filtered out. For the first time in his life, Webb had been attacked by severe cramp.

He lay in agony on the boat, his calves swollen and knotted with cramp, shivering like a man in a high fever. His face was dull and grey and his lips colourless. Hartley and his assistants helped him to a sofa in the cabin, rubbed his cold, twisted legs. Webb's stomach was wracked with pains and he was disappointed, deeply, bitterly disappointed. He'd lost the race and he'd lost his $1,000.

Throughout the day, more and more people arrived at the beach. Excursion parties from out of town swelled the crowd and the cliffs were black with holidaymakers, but all there was to see was Boyton monotonously paddling his way round the two buoys. Webb didn't see the end of the race but, lying bathed and rested in the Ocean House Hotel, the grandest in Newport, he couldn't have missed hearing the cheers as the victorious and considerably richer Boyton came ashore.

Two days later, in uncharacteristically combative language, Webb issued a challenge to Boyton through the pages of the *New York Herald*: 'Not being satisfied by the last trial for various reasons, I hereby challenge Captain Paul Boyton to swim against me for a similar stake and with the same privileges, he giving me the same allowance in the same ratio, for any number of miles from 10 to 20. Water to be agreed upon mutually.' Boyton accepted promptly.

At a time when Webb should have been resting, he entered on one of the busiest periods of his life. Hartley was organising a huge swimming marathon, the prize a gold medal called the Championship Medal of America, and the winner the man who swam the closest to 50 miles in a given period of time. He was also negotiating with swimmers from all over America for one-on-one competitions. Despite his defeat, Webb remained in good spirits, declaring that he was ready to meet with anyone but not all in the same season. 'When a man takes one of these very long swims it tires him out pretty well,' he told a reporter. 'A great deal of my trouble at Newport was due to that match being too soon after my swim from Sandy Hook to Manhattan Beach.'

Instead he tried to make up the $1,000 lost at Newport by a series of extravagant appearances at the Pemberton Hotel in Nantasket Beach, a town of summer lettings, famous for its red-roofed cottages, its long sandy beach and its clam bakes. The Pemberton Hotel was one of the largest and most luxurious in town. It had broad verandas and an 80-gallon swimming pool and was known for its spectacular fireworks. In the summer of 1879, the owner had hired a particularly brilliant pyrotechnist, Mr Morrits Blank, who created memorable displays by firing 50 rockets off at once and making coloured sparklers in the shape of a snake shimmer on the swimming pool. Against this background of noise and lights, Webb performed in the water, pretending to swim like a porpoise and a seal. He also did a

SPECIAL ANNOUNCEMENT!

The Most Interesting Exhibition Ever Witnessed on Nantasket Beach to take place September 4, 1879.

HAS BEEN WITNESSED BY MILLIONS IN EUROPE AND AMERICA.

10,000 MILES IN A RUBBER SUIT

Capt. PAUL BOYTON.

Who has Astonished the World by Swimming 10,000 Miles in a Rubber Suit.

—AND—

Capt. MATTHEW WEBB,

The Great English Champion Swimmer.

Will Contest for a Purse of $4,000 and the Championship of the World

—AT—

NANTASKET BEACH,

THURSDAY, SEPT. 4, 1879

Or the first fair day following.

The Swimmers will go into the water at 9 A. M from Nantasket Beach opposite Strawberry Hill, where the first buoy will be placed, and swim around the second buoy, which will be placed 1¼ mile distance, southerly toward the bend of the Beach, affording an opportunity for the multitude to witness the race its entire length and until the distance of 12½ miles has been accomplished."

The Mammoth Steamer EMPIRE STATE has been chartered for this occasion and will run from Litchfield's and Foster's Wharf(s) where special arrangements have been made to accommodate all who wish to witness this wonderful feat.

The fare for this day has been fixed at the low price of 50 Cents for the Round Trip and the following Time-table arranged:—

STEAMER LEAVE BOSTON.	LEAVE THE BEACH.
7.00 A. M.	7 ½ A. M.
8.30 "	8.30 "
9.00 "	9.30 "
9.30 "	10 00 "
10.30 "	10.30 "
11.00 "	11.00 "
11.30 "	12 00 M.
12.30 P. M.	12.30 P. M.
1.00 "	1.30 "
1.30 "	2 00 "
2.30 "	2 30 "
3.00 "	3.30 "
4.30 "	4.30 "
5.30 "	5.30 "
6.30 "	6.30 "
7.30 "	7.30 "
8.30 "	8 30 "
9.30 "	9.30 "

Litchfield's Wharf, 100 Atlantic Ave.

m31f　　　　H. T. LITCHFIELD, Supt.

Webb is all set to go head to head with his old enemy, Paul Boyton.

complicated routine where he imitated the movements of a paddle float, lying on his back, arms by his side, legs up at right angles. It was silly, it was undignified, a definite descent from his Channel-hero pedestal.

Meanwhile, huge posters were going up around Nantasket Beach announcing his match against Boyton, and there were newspaper adverts in the Boston papers. It was dubbed the 'Championship of the World' and trailed as 'The most interesting exhibition ever witnessed on Nantasket Beach'. Captain Boyton, who 'has astonished the World by Swimming 10,000 Miles in a Rubber Suit' would take on Captain Matthew Webb, 'the great English champion swimmer'. The prize was a staggering and unprecedented $4,000. Steamers were running special lines to take passengers to and from the beach – 50 cents for the round trip. Not even at his most flamboyant could Frederick Beckwith have dreamed up such a show.

It kept being postponed because the weather was so bad, but finally took place after a week of weary waiting on 6 September. This time there were three markers arranged in a line in the water – two boats and a buoy. The agreement was that Boyton paddled between all three points and Webb swam between two. The water was rough, and the boat carrying Webb's provisions was overturned even before the match started. A large crowd gathered but they must have been disappointed because the men were too far away to be seen clearly and it was pretty dull viewing anyway. Darkness fell

long before the race was completed. What happened after the race
was much more interesting.

In the first place, the referee, Thos R. Pickering, refused to
declare a winner though speculation put Webb in the lead by two
minutes. The following day, Pickering accused Webb of cheating,
alleging that on his last mile, he had taken advantage of the darkness
to swim in to the shore, run along the beach and then out to the
stake boat. He claimed he had two witnesses, young men who, while
strolling on the beach, had seen him do it.

Webb was furious. He prided himself on his honesty, had
written in his autobiography that as a child he'd 'had an instinctive
horror of a lie', declared himself an enemy of trickery, called Boyton
a fraud, and here he was, being accused of cheating. 'It's the most
infamous charge ever made against a professional man whose public
record is so well known,' he stormed. 'I never left the water until
I reached the stake boat. I did go in towards the shore because a
man in the police boat told me that if I could get close to the surf I
would strike a favourable tide. Four policemen who patrolled the
beach with lanterns testify that I did not come ashore, and yet the
referee, on a mere rumour, has reserved his decision.'

His manager, Hartley, weighed in with a powerful defence. How
could a man who had been swimming for eight hours just leave the
water and suddenly break into a run, he wanted to know. 'The thing
is absurd,' he fumed. 'No man could do it.' Referee bias was their
first suspicion, and easily confirmed, as it turned out that Pickering

was the father of Paul Boyton's fiancée. After being interviewed by Pickering, Webb's rage boiled over and he threatened to take legal advice. In the end, the deeply compromised referee declared the match a no-race and ordered the two men to swim it again.

What exactly happened? The full details never came out but certain facts were agreed on. The men entered the water at 11.30 on the morning of 6 September and during the day both moved at a steady pace through the sea, neither taking a decisive lead. When the race finished at just after nine o'clock in the evening, Webb was ahead, seated in the stake boat two minutes before Boyton paddled up. The American's supporters claimed they lost sight of Webb on the home stretch, presumably the period in which he was supposed to have gone ashore. In Webb's defence, there was the fact that electric lights were played on the water during the evening so Webb and Boyton could be seen from the boats if not from the beach. Boyton's future father-in-law was clearly the wrong man for the job of referee, and the two men who allegedly saw Webb on the beach never appeared to testify. On balance, Webb has to be acquitted of the charge. Nothing in his past suggested he was a cheat and why should he have changed overnight? Unfortunately, he wasn't given even the benefit of the doubt. Boyton was American, Webb was the foreigner. The Boston papers freely expressed their doubts about his win and his honesty.

There were no doubts about the endurance championship of the world. It was held on 14 September and Webb was soundly beaten by Von Schoening. He left the water after swimming just six miles, giving no explanation, though Henry Hartley said later that Webb 'had queer feelings in his stomach such as he had before being attacked with cramps in Newport'. The truth was he probably had no stomach for any further competition.

The second re-match between him and Boyton never came off. It was announced but Webb was worried about money and refused to go unless he was guaranteed $500 for appearing, a request the organisers refused to agree to. The money was probably an excuse. The long-awaited trial of strength between him and Boyton had ended in disaster and wounding accusations. Boyton rubbed salt in the wound with a letter to the *New York Herald*:

> The non-appearance of Captain Webb in Boston today to carry out the referee's decision on the last race between us, whereby it was to be swum again, compels me to claim the race as mine. In as much as both races I have had with him have terminated in an unsatisfactory manner, I hereby offer him the following proposition. I will, in my rubber suit, paddle fourteen miles while he is swimming ten miles, and will go in any water he may select, either publicly or privately, provided it is in North America. The match shall be for $1,000, each party to place 500 dollars in cash in the hands of the editor of the *New York Spirit of the Times*, who shall give the whole sum

to the winner of the race. You will observe that I am
offering him additional odds of a mile and half to his ten
miles beyond what I have ever offered him before and I
trust that the excessive odds will induce him to meet me
and abide by the decision of a referee who will not be
treated to the slander and abuse of either Webb or his
agent.

Webb did not bother to reply. Instead, he returned to England, not
actually disgraced, but defeated and defamed.

hatever Next!

In my opinion it is wicked for a man, merely for
the sake of gain or of notoriety, to risk his life.
_____ *Matthew Webb, 1879*

The 40 ft-long glass tank had once been home to a baby whale from
Labrador. The poor creature had perished in the overheated
environment of the Royal Westminster Aquarium. For the next two
and a half days, the tank would be home to Matthew Webb. In March
1880 he had accepted a bet of £100 to £20 that he could spend 60
hours in the tank. Whether he would prove to be as popular a draw
as the whale remained to be seen.

At first it looked unlikely. Webb stripped for action in a jersey,
black drawers and white socks but it was 10.30 in the morning, half
an hour past the advertised start time, and the room was almost
empty. As he mounted the small box that served as a makeshift
diving board, Webb seemed embarrassed and unsure of himself. He
made a speech, speaking vaguely in short, jerky sentences: he wasn't

attempting the feat for the love of the thing, he told the near-empty hall, but for money. Perhaps he realised how unattractive that sounded because he added that he still hoped it would prove useful in promoting the art of swimming. With that, he prepared himself to dive into the water but before he could move, an elderly gentleman called out to him: 'Are you doing this for money?' 'Yes,' Webb replied. 'Then here is a sovereign for you, will you have it?' his questioner wanted to know. 'No, I've got no pockets,' said Webb and flopped into the water and began swimming.

The sovereign was an insult, but everything about the event was tawdry. Once in the water, Webb didn't even pretend to take what he was doing seriously. He chatted idly to the few bystanders as he flipped round the tank until the organisers put a stop to that by posting a notice asking visitors 'not to speak to the man at the wheel'. From then on, he swam in silence and when, after 50 minutes, he turned to float on his back, he saw that everyone but the referee had vanished. The next 59 hours must have yawned before him.

Around him sounded the various exotic wildlife the aquarium specialised in exhibiting – singing birds, talking parrots – and, every hour, a clock sounded. But the noise Webb would have wanted to hear – the cheers and chatter of an excited audience – was missing. By midday, it was clear that his latest venture was a failure. There was hardly anyone there to see Boy Baker float Webb's lunch of meatballs across the water to him on a table specially built for the event. A few people turned up around three o'clock in time to see his tea served up to him in the same way, but most of them didn't stay for long; they wandered off into the main part of the building to look at the animals or to watch the daring exploits of the Brothers Dare, or listen to some lively singing by the Casetti sisters, four young women from the Tyrol, or laugh at the antics of the musical clowns, the Brothers Raynor and Kaouly, the juggler. When those attractions palled, there was always the billiards match. From being the centre of attention, Webb had quite literally become a side show, tucked away in an annexe, a little marvel among newer marvels. The strength of long-distance swimming is in its steadiness, the application, over and over again, of rhythmic powerful movements. Unfortunately for Webb, that same quality made for very monotonous entertainment. But he kept at it, alternately swimming and floating, and when he heard that Parliament was due to be dissolved by Easter, quipped that he would be dissolved himself long before that.

Just before midnight, the aquarium emptied and most of the lights in the building were turned out. All the birds went to sleep except for the bald-headed geese of the Ganges who croaked throughout the long night. The only people left were the referee, a few members of the press, Baker and Willie Beckwith. They stayed on, drinking champagne, whisky and brandy, eating steaks and chops, and watching Webb swimming very slowly up and down the tank. They all agreed that it was very dull work.

Things perked up slightly when a sporting peer, Lord Aylesford, and some friends paid a visit and one of them joined Webb for a short while in the tank. Webb played to this mini-crowd by floating on his back and smoking a cigar. After they vanished, monotony descended again, the only breaks being for Webb's meal times and when some people tried to climb the walls in order to get a free glimpse. The onlookers struggled to stay awake.

At four o'clock, the cockatoos squawked into life and still Webb kept swimming. At six, the singing birds woke up and he was still there. At 7.35 a.m. the doors of the aquarium were opened and some of the building's employees came to see him, but it wasn't until ten o'clock that a member of the public turned up.

Webb remained in the tank all day long, floating on his back, drinking a glass of malt and a cup of green tea. It was obvious that he was desperate for sleep as he kept trying to doze off in the water, a quite impossible task, but when asked, he always said he was fine. A doctor was sent for and his friends persuaded him to leave the water for a while. After 38 hours, 52 minutes and 10 seconds, he climbed jauntily out of the tank and, while laughing and joking with his friends, allowed the doctor to examine him. There was chafing at the nape of his neck and on the inside of his legs but apart from that his skin seemed barely affected. To the amazement of his friends, the doctor pronounced Webb's pulse perfectly normal and his temperature only slightly below. Webb applied some spermaceti oil to the chafing and then, 21 minutes and 30 seconds later, slipped back into the water.

The second half of any long swim is always better than the first and the hours slipped away. Visitors came and went. At one point a macaw escaped and had to be rescued after it fluttered into one of the tanks. Webb ate his meals on the water – minced beef, coffee, sole served with a spicy sauce. He smoked his cigars. Three Zulu princesses came to have a look at the captain and were amazed to hear what was happening. Lord Aylesford came back. More coffee and beef tea, and then the clock struck the start of the last hour. The room began to fill. Throughout the last hour, the bell sounded every five minutes, counting down to the end. Webb, who had been conserving his strength by just treading water, now rallied and with the last of his energy, began turning somersaults. At exactly 10.30, he turned in the water one last time, swam to the side and climbed up the ladder. He had to be helped to his dressing room and was then taken home and put immediately to bed.

So 1880 opened badly for Webb. He hit a new low in his life with that 60-hour swim at the Westminster Aquarium. As a spectacle it bored the public, and it depleted his physical resources more that it increased his financial ones.

In April, he married. He was 32, the same age as his father had been on his wedding day, and, like his father, he chose a much younger woman. Her name was Madeleine Kate Chaddock and he had met her at a ball in London; she was just 20 years old, the daughter of a gentleman who lived in the then suburb of Baron's Court. Friends described her as small, with a refined appearance, and she wore her hair drawn smoothly back from a well-shaped head. The marriage certificate records Webb as a 'Master Mariner', although he hadn't been on a ship for seven years. That must have brought home to him how little he had moved on and how far he was from building a new role for himself. The wedding, which was held at the Church of St Andrews in West Kensington, was quiet, with just a tiny notice inserted in the *Daily Telegraph*. The bride and groom were clearly very fond of each other. Webb took her with him on his exhibition travels round England; on one occasion she had her own moment of celebrity when she launched a lifeboat. She called him Mat and thought he was simply splendid. In some ways, though, the marriage was bad for him. It forced him to think and plan and earn for two people, and for three when Madeleine became pregnant. He seemed willing to take seriously any idea, however far-fetched or unlikely. In July, he was listening to a plan for a mass Channel swim and, in August, he lowered his standing a few more notches with another marathon tank flotation, this time in the aquarium at Scarborough. He was sandwiched between the skipping rope performances of Mademoiselle Marian Bosanquet and Little Louie with her powers of second sight. Webb spent 74 hours in the water but it was Little Louie who was booked for a second week.

There were disappointments everywhere. He lost a good friend and a press ally when Frank Buckland from *Land and Water* died at the beginning of 1881. And his health was beginning to falter. A six-day swim at the Lambeth Baths and a 16-mile contest against Willie Beckwith in a 20-yard king tank at the Royal Aquarium exhausted him. His eyes flared up and his left shoulder began to ache on the long swims. He was 33, too old to be competing against the 22-year-old Beckwith, and a combination of long, arduous swims and bouts of high living was taking its toll. He was swimming too much but probably felt he had to keep going: he needed the money badly. That summer his wife gave birth to a son, another Matthew, and he had no other means of supporting his family. Friends noticed a new recklessness about his behaviour now but, given his physical condition, to agree to a five-hour outdoor swim in Lancashire in October was nothing short of madness.

His opponent, Dr G. A. Jennings, was known to the swimming world as a man with ambitions to swim the Channel and a complete absence of the ability to come anywhere near it. He had plenty of stamina and had managed a number of long-distance swims in both lakes and the sea but he swam such a slow, rolling, clumsy side stroke that he would have frozen to death before he was half-way across the Channel. But he was a man obsessed, always trying to drum up interest in an attempt and writing long, rambling letters to the press, calling on the government to support Channel swimming. He was a poor opponent for Webb, his swimming so weak that he was bound to lose, but his reputation as an eccentric would make Webb's victory a hollow one. Agreeing to meet him was bad judgement on Webb's part, but even worse was agreeing to meet him at Hollingsworth

Lake near Rochdale in Lancashire on 1 October. It was a popular spot for swimming contests, the site of several big races, and J. B. Johnson had swum there, but not in the autumn when the temperature of the water was below 60 degrees. Robert Watson thought it was suicidal. 'Like swimming through water impregnated with ice,' he said, and he always maintained that the event stood out as 'the most inhuman and useless form of sport' it had ever been his misfortune to witness. Webb, who had once regarded Watson as the expert on swimming matters, was deaf to common sense. He took the contest seriously, training for long hours in the Clapham and Brixton Baths, where the water was heated to 60 degrees. Still critical but loyal, Watson and Baker agreed to go and take care of Webb as usual. And so, for a stake of £100, he prepared to put his health and his reputation once more on the line.

The course at Hollingsworth Lake was simple: 110 yards long and divided from the rest of the lake by a rope. It was moderately well sheltered from the wind. The Lancashire and Yorkshire Railway Company had arranged special trains to the spot during the day, but they were to be sorely disappointed by the take-up. Hardly anyone showed up.

The sun was shining when the two men took their places on the diving board, but the temperature of the water was only 54 degrees. Jennings seemed the better bet, standing 5 ft 10½ in and weighing just over 14 stone. Webb had lost weight again and weighed only 13 stone, a stone and a half below his Channel weight, fat he could ill afford to do without if his body was going to be able to withstand the cold of the lake. Both men looked very strange. Webb's body was a bright yellow from porpoise oil and resin, while dubbin, blacking and grease gave Jennings the appearance of a chimney sweep. The contest was simple: whoever swam the greatest distance in five hours was the winner.

When water is cold, it is best to get in quickly. Webb went in first, swimming through the icy lake towards the first buoy. Within minutes, it was patently clear who would win. Despite regular training at the Tunbridge Wells Baths near his home, Jennings had failed to improve his style. His side stroke was painfully slow and he rolled about in the water like a porpoise; he was so unco-ordinated he got his feet tangled in the rope and it took him one hour and 25 minutes to cover his first mile; Webb did it in 42 minutes 49 seconds. In the next five hours, Webb increased his lead, but only a sadist could have enjoyed watching them. Webb's speed was good; he was now a fast as well as a skilled swimmer, but he was in agony from the cold. His limbs became so numb he could no longer hold his head above the surface, and kept choking from the water in his nose and mouth. At one point it looked as if he was becoming unconscious, and a frightened Watson rowed his boat near him and called out, asking if he was all right. Webb replied but Watson realised, to his horror, that he was speaking to an imaginary person; he was hallucinating. Boy Baker giving him old ale only made him worse. Jennings, on the other hand, seemed perfectly happy in the icy water, rolling away, taking at least three seconds between each stroke and calling out to his friends. He looked as if he was enjoying himself.

Twelve minutes before the five hours were up, Webb became so delirious he lost all sense of direction. Instead of swimming to the buoy, he turned round when he was 20 yards away from it. Half a minute before the race was officially over, he was at the diving board, a move which technically lost him the race. But nobody was thinking of that then. Poor Webb couldn't move. He stood in the bitterly cold water, his head resting on the step of the diving board, and vomited weakly. Gently, Baker and Watson coaxed him out and supported him up the small hill to the dressing room. He moved like a man on crutches, walking straddle-legged. He had swum five miles, three laps and 660 yards, Jennings three miles, seven laps and 1,540 yards, but the latter sprang neatly up the diving board and bowed to the few people watching. He was no swimmer but he certainly had a remarkable tolerance to the cold.

Prostrate in the dressing room, Webb lay babbling like a baby. Baker worked on him for half an hour, wiping off the porpoise oil, pouring warm water over his frozen body and forcing hot coffee down his throat. Even when he was restored to rationality, Webb was still very weak. A week later he still hadn't recovered and, according to Watson, he never really did. 'The race subsequently had a very serious effect upon Webb's constitution,' he recalled. 'He never seemed to me like the Webb of old. His career also had a downward tendency and the grand athlete of 1875, the idol of the fashionable world and swimmers generally, had almost played his last card, and after reaching the pinnacle of fame commenced henceforth the journey down the hill of life with astonishing and lamentable alacrity.'

Webb began casting around almost wildly for his next project. He had a mad correspondence in the pages of the *Sporting Life* with Willie Beckwith about another six-day swimming contest. Beckwith wanted it to be for a maximum of 14 hours a day; Webb wanted unlimited time. With charming understatement, Beckwith called the prospect of swimming all day and all night for six days 'rather stiff', but gamely agreed. 'If Captain knows a suitable place for about 20 hours each day, I will oblige him. I think this is a fair offer.' Fair or not, Webb was having none of it; it was all or nothing for him. He replied: 'In answer to Beckwith's last letter, offering to swim a six days' match with me, the hours limited to 20 a day, I think he might just as well leave out the four hours' rest, and let each man swim as long as he can during the six days and nights. This will be the fairest test of speed and endurance, and no other terms will suit me.' Beckwith didn't reply and Webb allowed the subject to drop, but he was still hell-bent on proving himself in some way, yet he was increasingly picking contests that other swimmers thought frivolous and the public found dull.

Once again he turned his attention back to the United States, and in the summer of 1882 he left England when the swimming season was at its height and sailed to New York. He didn't fare that much better than on his last visit. On 1 July he gave himself the title of 'long-distance champion of England' and swam a five-mile race in the sea at Brighton Beach against the 'champion ocean swimmer of America', who was a good-natured railroad engineer from Brooklyn called George Wade. The two men swam through a strong tide and a lightning storm, Wade initially in the lead but Webb overtaking him on the home stretch and reaching the finish a minute ahead. The stake money was advertised as being $1,000, but in fact the race had been organised by the owners of the bars and restaurants along the front and the large sum of money was imaginary. Another five-mile race between Webb and 22 competitors at Nantasket Beach saw him the winner but in a contest so badly organised that nobody seriously believed the times quoted. In fact, neither race had any real claim to being a sporting event.

They did, however, still look a lot more like sport than did the swimming exhibitions he gave that summer at Nantasket Beach. His speciality was holding aloft a fiery torch and taking a 50 ft dive into a sea glittering with electric lights. But the lowest point was his 'living death' exhibition at the Horticultural Hall Building in Boston. The city had never seen anything like it – a man prepared to spend 128½ hours – over five days – in a tank. It was a rerun, only longer, of his Westminster and Scarborough Aquariums exhibitions. The Bostonians seemed to enjoy it, large crowds attending every day for the dubious pleasure of watching Webb swim around and eat his meals off a tray floated across the water to him. It drained him of energy, his skin flared up into ugly red blotches and his hands and feet looked bleached, but he remained cheerful. He talked nonsense to anyone who would listen, saying things that simply couldn't be true. He was not in the least tired, he claimed, at least not by the water. He did find the presence of so many people a bit fatiguing, he admitted. If he could have slept on the water, he said, it would have been better, but people had paid to see him move and move he must. If he had been allowed to sleep, he could have kept it up for another week.

The way in which he tried to pretend the event had some real merit was pitiful. 'I wished to show them that a knowledge of the water was the best life-preserver in case of accident,' he said. 'I am willing to sacrifice myself to a certain extent to do this. Perhaps I have miscalculated the extent of my power in this large and unoccupied field of missionary effect. But I hope not.' The awkwardness he'd displayed at Westminster was long gone; the shame of a thing decreases with each time it is done. A new cockiness had entered his manner; he refused even to admit that the five-day immersion had exhausted him. 'After leaving it on Sunday morning, I went to bed, slept soundly for eight hours and after breakfast took a five-mile walk and felt refreshed after it,' he bragged unconvincingly.

As for real racing, he seemed keen to avoid any proper challenges, as the sporting journal *New York Turf, Field and Form* rather sourly pointed out: 'Captain Webb does not seem prepared to meet swimmers of recognised merit.'

The 'living death' exhibition had earned him $1,000 and, had he been prepared to continue down the stunts route, he could have made a decent living. But he still wanted to be thought of as a proper swimmer, a man with a serious purpose, who showed others the importance of swimming.

In November, his wife had their second child, a girl they named Helen. Madeleine may have been so preoccupied with her children that she failed to notice that her husband was living in a fantasy world. He was now dabbling with the idea of being an inventor, hinting that he'd found a 'new method of propulsion in the water' which would 'lay out Captain Boyton's contrivances for the same purpose'. What it was, if it ever existed, remained a mystery. Nor did anyone ever see his ingenious bicycle, his swimming apparatus or his flying machine, which flapped like a seagull. Apparently he fell and broke his nose trying the last one out.

The following year, Webb arranged to swim 20 miles in the Lambeth Baths against Beckwith for £100. Webb didn't stand a chance. He was 35 and the previous five years had been badly spent. He was pale and drawn and, at 11 st 6 lb, much lighter than he'd ever been. Beckwith was 10 years younger and in the peak of condition, and he hadn't spent the previous year ruining his health in silly exhibitions. The minute they entered the water, Beckwith began to pull away from Webb. He covered the first mile a minute faster and, at the end of five miles, he was seven laps in front. Even a 12-minute absence by Beckwith, who was feeling slightly ill, didn't give Webb enough advantage. Beckwith returned and soon easily passed him. Webb swam 17 miles and left the water; his attendant, Baker, begged him not to get back in that night. On Tuesday morning, the two men began by swimming close together for a mile and a half. Then Webb fell behind and it soon became clear that something was wrong. He kept getting out of the water and then, to the horror of his attendants, he started spitting blood. 'I'm not going to kill myself to please anybody,' he told them and left the baths.

For a fortnight, Webb was unable to leave his bed; the diagnosis was 'congestion of the lungs', the Victorians' term for pneumonia. As he lay there, with plenty of time to contemplate the ruin of his health and his reputation, he received a letter from his brother, Dr Thomas Webb. Thomas wrote affectionately and anxiously, begging him to give up the long-distance swims. He'd heard about Lambeth and was alarmed. He warned his brother that at the age of 35, his muscles would not be so powerful and that a man's body gradually deteriorates after the age of 30. Webb did not reply.

Two months later, he appeared at a race night at the Battersea Baths, where Watson was acting as referee. Webb had been engaged to open the event, swim and give away the prize. Watson could hardly recognise his friend. He looked ill and his greeting, 'Holloa, Bob', was spoken in a dull and unhappy way. And he was desperate to avoid any swimming.

'I say, old man, I'm very ill and my doctor forbids me to swim tonight,' he told Watson. 'I want you to get me out of the difficulty. I want you to see if the proprietor of the bath will allow me to do something else, for swimming is out of the question, and I don't want him to deduct any of the money he has arranged to give me.' Watson pleaded successfully with the owner and Webb merely appeared to the strains of 'See the Conquering Hero Comes', repeated most of his long-ago speech at St James's Hall and gave away the prize.

That seems to have been the last time he took any precaution for his health. He had up his sleeve a scheme so huge, a plan so extravagant that, if he pulled it off, it would eclipse everything – even his Channel crossing.

Chapter 10

A Rum Bit of Water

Nature was at once stamped upon my heart, an image of Beauty; to remain there, changeless and indelible, until its pulses cease to beat, for ever.

_____ American Notes, *Charles Dickens, 1842*

The more improbable the situation and the greater the demands made, the more sweetly the blood flows later in release from all that tension. The possibility of danger serves merely to sharpen his awareness and control. And perhaps this is the rationale of all risky sports: You deliberately raise the ante of effort and concentration in order, as it were, to clear your mind of trivialities. It's a small-scale model for

living, but with a difference. Unlike your routine
life, where mistakes can usually be recouped and
some kind of compromise patched up, your
actions, for however brief a period, are deadly
serious.

_____ The Savage God: A Study of Suicide,
A. Alvarez, 1971

Once, the great lakes of northern America were all one, locked
together in an almighty ice lake. Then when the climate warmed
up some time between 1,000 and 10,000 BC, the ice melted and
the water levels rose. With a roar, Lake Algonquin pushed through
the rock and fell into Lake Iroquois, 250 feet below. And so the
Niagara Falls were born, the third largest in the world; two mighty
waterfalls, one on the American side – staggering at 288 feet high
and 491 feet wide – and the Canadian Horseshoe Falls – shorter
at 176 feet but 2,194 feet wide, literally a wall of water. From the
falls, the Niagara River foams milky-white for 1,000 feet of rapids
before it is checked by sharp, jutting rocks and enters an enormous
whirlpool, a quarter of a mile in diameter. Here the water swirls
violently round in a clockwise direction before surging out and
onwards at 39 miles an hour. The local Indian tribe, the Neutrals,
called the Niagara River the Thunder of the Waters and buried
their dead on one of its islands. It is a magical sight, one of the
wonders of the natural world, but not in the least the sort of river

a normal man would contemplate swimming. But that is exactly what Webb proposed to do. He called it 'a rum bit of water'.

Watson and Beckwith were appalled. Over and over again Beckwith begged Webb not to attempt it, but he wouldn't listen. Watson tried his influence. 'From what I hear, you will never come out alive,' he told him and Webb replied: 'I don't care. I want money and I must have it.'

He was indifferent to the risk of dying. 'We must all face it one day,' he said. 'I have been near it many a time, quite as close as they say a man is at Niagara, and got clean away.' Perhaps he was thinking of his struggle in the Atlantic when he jumped off the *Russia* to save Michael Hynes. 'I know I am going in for something terribly big and must take my chance,' he said.

Watson looked his friend full in the face and was shocked by what he saw. The deterioration of Webb's physical and emotional condition was complete. Watson recalled in his memoirs: 'As we stood face to face, I compared the fine handsome sailor who first spoke to me about swimming, with the broken-spirited and terribly altered appearance of the man who courted death in the whirlpool rapids. His object was not suicide, but money and imperishable fame.'

Webb was not the first person to try for a dubious sort of immortality at Niagara. This one-time battleground of Indians, French priests and Canadian skin traders had become a playground, a honeymoon spot and the primary port of call in

North America for daredevils, conmen, suicides, sensation-seekers and nutters.

Sightseeing came to Niagara in the 1820s, first sedately with newlyweds, then, after the opening of railway links in 1853, exuberantly in a torrent of daytrippers. By 1860, Niagara saw over 50,000 visitors every summer. The American side was (and still is) hideously bloated with factories, but on the Canadian side visitors strolled down the front, past hotels, shops, booths, taverns and Indian tents, looking for the best view of the falls. Anyone stepping off the train was seized by a hack driver who got a commission from the hotel he drove them to. The place was full of gamblers, hustlers and touts. Years later, Rupert Brooke called Niagara 'the central home and breeding place for all the touts on earth . . . who have no apparent object in the world but just purely, simply, merely, indefatigably – to tout'. He was right – and it had always been like that.

Niagara had the best of things and the worst. The falls had a grandeur no amount of tackiness could mask. You could board the *Maid of the Mist* and sail so close to the falls that it became impossible to hear yourself think, never mind speak, and the air turned into a fine mist. Or you could pay 50 cents and take a cable car to the edge of the boiling whirlpool. And a dollar would give you a hired waterproof and a guide to the cave of the winds where you stood, drenched and overwhelmed, behind a white sheet of falling water. For free, you could stand on the huge spanning suspension bridge and look down, dizzyingly, into the churning waters below.

Yet there was also a sleaziness in the heart of Niagara, a whiff of dishonesty and more than a hint of cruelty. In 1827, three hotel owners attempted to drum up trade by sending a leaky ship over the falls with live animals on board. This was watched, apparently, by over 10,000 people and it put Niagara on the map as a place where extraordinary things happened. In 1829, Sam Patch, a 22-year-old from Rhode Island, became the first Niagara daredevil when he dived into the river from one of the islands and survived. In the late 1850s, the great tightrope walker Blondin crossed Niagara several times, sometimes pushing a wheelbarrow, supporting a basket of peaches on his head and carrying his manager on his back. Bellini, another tightrope walker, upped the ante by diving into the river as well as crossing it. He survived that fall but in a similar performance in 1886, he broke his ribs on impact with the water; he died jumping off a bridge in London two years later. Niagara was used to showmen so, when in June 1883, Matthew Webb appeared in town, announcing his intention of swimming down the river, no one batted an eyelid.

It was as if a switch had been flicked in Webb's mind. Usually taciturn and rather private, he was now voluble and confiding. He flaunted himself about Niagara, talking about his project to anyone who would listen and soliciting bets. He would get into a boat and sail out to just below the suspension bridge, to the point where

the water was about 95 feet deep. That way, he explained in all
seriousness, he would avoid the two jagged rocks and he could stay
away from the centre of the river. Certain death there, he agreed,
but just below the suspension bridge was fine. He would jump
from the boat and swim down the river. If the water was too rough,
he would dive deep down and come up only now and again to
breathe – and to show off his swimming. The whirlpool was
obviously a worry, and he thought that when he came near it, it
would probably take him about two hours to resist its pull. On
second thoughts, maybe three. After that, he would head for the
Canadian shore, but if the current was too strong for him, he
would simply go with it and land himself at Lewiston, eight miles
away on the American side. He'd given some thought to his outfit
too. What could be more suitable than the red swimming trunks
in which he'd swum the Channel?

There were only two possible responses to such madness:
disbelief or a dire warning – and he received plenty of both. Locals
came forward with all the stories they knew about Niagara and its
dangers. They told him that in the whirlpool the water is
sometimes 400 feet deep, not 95, and that 20 ft-long logs are
sucked down and forced to stand on end like ship's masts. And if
a human being was sucked in there it could be months before the
body was seen. The body floated there, swirling round and round
in the fierce current before chance drew it into just the right eddy
to be spat out and bob to the surface. They told him how, a couple

of years earlier, a boy who was paddling around in the water was sucked into the rapids and had his head cut off. And about the girl who tumbled into the river from the suspension bridge and the force of the water tore off all her clothes except her stockings. Didn't he know that 80 people had died in the rapids? John P. Hathorn, one of the men who built the *Maid of the Mist*, a man who knew the river better than almost anyone, described Webb's project as the most foolhardy thing he'd ever heard of. 'A man might as well jump off the top of the Tribune building and expect to strike the sidewalk unhurt as try to swim over that place.'

And why was Webb doing all this? For money, he said. He was lost to reason, high on adrenalin and excitement, but he had ceased to pretend to be anything other than what he was – a stuntman. There was no more high-minded waffle about life-saving and promoting the valuable sport of swimming. He stood there, as bold as brass, and told the truth – he was in it for the money. There were discussions taking place with the railroad companies, he said; they would pay him $10,000 if he was successful. They knew a good deal when they saw it, he boasted; they were going to lay on special trains to bring the hundreds and thousands of people who wanted to see his swim. And he was talking to the owners of the Niagara Falls Hotel, asking them to pay him $1,000, easily recouped from the extra guests his swim would bring. Most of his listeners took it all with a pinch of salt, watched him go and forgot about him. Just another mad Englishman, they probably told themselves, as crazy as the one they called the 'Hermit of the Falls', that strange but harmless loner who lived on one of the islands in Niagara and wandered about at night, the one who drowned in the river.

Webb spent the rest of June and most of July with Madeleine and the children at Nantasket Beach where he'd hired a cottage. He chose Nantasket because he thought the breakers there were rough enough to prepare him for Niagara. His health was better than it had been for some time, and he'd gained some of his lost weight. If he hadn't been planning on swimming Niagara, you could have said that he'd become almost prudent because he was living quietly, drinking no spirits and paying attention to his diet. When he wasn't training, he spent his time teaching Madeleine to swim and playing with two-year-old Matthew and baby Helen. Yet even then, there were hints of mental disintegration. A holidaymaker near the cottage remembered Webb as being determined that his little son would grow up to be fearless and so, to toughen him up, he would wrap him up in a hammock and swing him high into the air. His mind turned constantly on the question of proving yourself.

He talked about money all the time. He found himself a new manager, a Frederick Kyle, he discussed exhibition possibilities and other money-making schemes. He even confided in him about his most recent inventions, two new methods for propelling boats. 'I wish this exhibition business was over,' he told Kyle. 'There is not much money in it, and no fun, but won't there be a lot of money in these new ideas of mine when I get them patented?' 'There must be some money in an exhibition here,' he said on another occasion. 'I think we had better get one up later.'

He dismissed Madeleine's worries about Niagara, telling her there was very little danger. 'The Americans don't have much of an idea of water,' he claimed, and he'd repeat one of his favourite sayings: 'A man could live in surf where a boat would die.' At one point he told her that he was thinking of swimming the rapids once a week; it would be a good speculation. Amazingly, Madeleine seems to have believed it all, but it should be said in her defence that she was still young, only 24, had no knowledge of America or swimming and had never seen the rapids.

Webb had moments of sanity. In early July, his wife wrote to her parents that he had given up the Niagara project, but on 23 July he left her alone with the children in Nantasket and departed for Niagara with Kyle. Webb was bouncing with confidence, promising to telegraph her the minute he was out of the river. He and Kyle arrived in Niagara on the morning of Tuesday 24 July and checked into the Clifton House Hotel, one of the largest in town.

Dressed in a light-grey suit and concealing whatever turmoil he felt under a relaxed and cheerful manner, Webb strolled out to hire a boatman to row him out into the river. At the offices of the *Niagara Falls Gazette* he posted a bulletin which read: 'Captain Webb will swim the whirlpool rapids at 4 o'clock this afternoon', and a ripple of excitement began to spread through the town. An old sea captain heard the news and approached Webb. Did he realise how difficult it would be to swim the Niagara River, how rash a venture it was? Webb listened politely and, when the man turned away, said to Kyle: 'Well-meaning old cove, isn't he?' He was taking a breezy view of difficulties. To everyone who warned him that day, he always said, with the utmost good humour: 'He thinks he knows a lot about the water, don't he?' A Niagara boatman, Jack McCloy, agreed to take him out into the river, and he then returned to the hotel where a number of reporters were waiting to interview him.

First, he confirmed that he was actually going to swim the rapids. 'Yes,' he told the reporter from the *New York Herald*. 'I am going to swim the whirlpool rapids, and I will say that is about the angriest bit of water in the world. They are rough, I tell you, and the whirlpool is a grand one, but I think I am strong enough and skilled enough to go through alive. The people at Niagara Falls tell me that I will be simply committing suicide.' How on earth did he imagine he was going to do it, the reporter wanted to know? Webb broke into such a full and detailed explanation about how he was proposing to risk his life that it would have been funny if it had not been pitiful. 'I'll explain my plan,' he said.

At the time appointed I will leap into the river and float into the rapids. Of course I will make the attempt to go forward, but the fearful speed of the water will carry me through. When the water gets very bad I will go under the surface and remain beneath until I am compelled to come up for breath. That will be pretty often, I'll wager. When I strike the whirlpool I will strike out with all my strength and try to keep away from the suck hole in the centre. I will begin with the breast stroke and then use overhand stroke. My life will then depend upon my muscles and my breath, with a little touch of science behind them. It may take me two or three hours to get out of the whirlpool, which is about a quarter-mile long. When I do get through, I will try to land on the Canadian side, but if the current is too swift, as I think it is, I will keep onto Lewiston on the American side.

In return for risking the danger, he would receive $10,000 from the railroad companies. The money was his sole motivation. Later a reporter from the local paper, the *Niagara Falls Gazette*, got the truth out of him. There was no money in it at all. Webb admitted that when he came to drum up interest in June, he had expected to make a small fortune, but the railway companies had refused to sponsor him so now he was doing it simply for what he called 'the credit of his good name'.

'They did not think that I would attempt it,' he told the reporter. 'I said I would and am doing it because no other man has ever made the attempt. I am determined my reputation shall not suffer.' He didn't want too much publicity, he said, quite mendaciously, because that would only benefit the railroads. After his swim, he would return to England with his family; he'd already bought the tickets and expected to sail on Saturday.

Everything he said pointed to his mental confusion. The glib way he dismissed the danger, the pretence that he didn't want publicity, the belief that his reputation would be enhanced by going in the river – it all added up to a man going out of his mind. He was like a manic depressive in an up cycle.

After his interviews, he made his will, leaving all his property to his wife, ate a hearty lunch, changed his shirt and then asked to speak to the hotel owner. Webb had several valuable items he wanted to leave with him and Mr Coburn agreed. They were a watch with the inscription: 'Presented to Captain Matthew Webb on the occasion of his having performed the unprecedented feat of swimming the English Channel. By a few of his friends and admirers. London, September 9 1875', with a seal marked 'M.W.'; and a Maltese cross engraved: 'To Capt. Matthew Webb by the Victoria Athletic Club Stoke Upon Trent. Dec. 22nd 1875'. There's something poignant about his concern for the safety of these two treasures from his past fame.

At about four p.m., Kyle got into a hack and set off for the Canadian side of the whirlpool, while another man, a Mr Davy, headed over the bridge to the American side. Webb walked down alone from the Clifton Hotel to the ferry landing. Whether they had believed him or not, some people still thought it was worth paying a visit to the river at the appointed time. Small groups were making their way towards the suspension bridge, gathering in huddles along the river bank between the bridge and the whirlpool.

Jack McCloy and his wife were waiting with a small fishing boat, near the *Maid of the Mist* embarcation point. Mrs McCloy was clearly concerned; she'd come along to ask Webb if he thought he would see his wife and children again. He replied confidently: 'I hope to.' She obviously appealed to something in him because, while McCloy got the boat ready, he told her about his family. They were all at Nantasket Beach, he said, his wife, his son and his baby daughter. He would meet them there in a few days' time.

Then he stepped into the boat and McCloy began to steer it out towards the suspension bridge; Webb was still chatting away happily. His mind was in the past: he described his Channel swim in detail and bragged that since then he'd made $25,000 in swimming exhibitions.

'How much have you got left?' asked McCloy.

'About $15,000,' was the reply.

'Then you'd better let me pull you ashore and go on a $15,000 spree rather than try to go through this. You cannot do it. It is sure death.'

Webb was already undressing, stripping down to his red trunks. When McCloy told him he wouldn't need his clothes again, he only laughed and asked the boatman to meet him just below the whirlpool with his clothes and some blankets as he wanted to go to Boston the following day. And now, would McCloy please row him as far as he dared into the middle of the river?

From the bridge the onlookers watched the tiny boat stop. Webb stood up, said goodbye to McCloy, paused briefly in the prow of the boat and then plunged head first into the water. From the banks a great cheer went up.

He went into the river at exactly 4.32. A minute later, he surfaced and McCloy could see him: he was swimming powerfully downriver. He looked quite untroubled, as if he was simply enjoying a pleasant swim. He swam under the railroad bridge. Below, the river narrowed, the waters rising violently up in the centre. Then he was in the rapids. For one dizzying second, his body was thrust upright, poised on top of a high wave and then he was gone, diving under the water and out of sight. The spectators on the bridge groaned. Seconds passed, long, tense seconds, and then he was spotted again, bobbing and tossing on the surface, at least 150 yards from the spot where he had gone down. Twice, three times he was dragged under the water and rose again. The water was pushing him downstream at a furious pace. Carriages raced down the river bank, people craned to see through opera glasses.

He was no longer in control; the rapids were forcing him straight ahead. A quarter of a mile from the whirlpool, a bend in the river made the water smack the banks violently. Ahead was the worst yet – the whirlpool, a shrieking, hissing vortex. To those on the bridge, Webb was now a mere speck, a tiny dot of humanity lost in the heaving waters. Suddenly he threw up his right arm and went down again.

On the bridge they waited, their eyes eagerly scanning the water, wondering where he would reappear. A quarter of an hour passed and no sign of Webb. Downriver, Kyle waited for Webb to swim ashore. Half an hour passed. No Webb. The crowd on the bridge had gone home. The show was over, and the river rolled on. At six o'clock, a carriage appeared and Kyle saw Davy climb out. Webb hadn't made it to the American side either. Kyle refused to give up hope and drove down to nearby Queenstown to see if Webb had been swept past both him and Davy and landed there instead.

Back in Niagara, the rumour mill began to grind into action. A lot of attention was paid to Felix Nassoiy, a clerk who kept a small boat on the river near the *Maid of the Mist* landing. He and a friend had been out on the river when McCloy's boat appeared in sight and had watched Webb jump, before steering their boat within 30 feet of him. Webb, they said, called out hello and told them he would be back at the hotel soon. This story is almost certainly make-believe, as Webb would have been swept along too quickly for conversation and would have had too much to do to stay afloat to talk to anyone. But Nassoiy claimed to be the last person to speak to Webb and that evening he was listened to. So too was a Mr

Pomeroy, who worked for a newspaper called the *Bridge Journal*. He claimed to be the last man to see Webb. He said he had seen the swimmer just after he had passed through the rapids, but as to whether he was dead or alive then he couldn't say.

The ghouls were out in force, speculating that if his body hadn't been torn to pieces, it was still in the whirlpool. Bets were placed as to whether it would ever turn up. Some claimed they could see the head of a man, turning endlessly in the whirlpool. One cynic insisted he didn't believe that Webb had gone into the water at all. He thought it was all a con, that Webb had pretended to swim Niagara and was now holed up somewhere downriver. He was sure he would turn up soon enough and claim it as a big success. Others claimed to have heard Webb say that it was all or nothing with him, that he would swim the rapids and the whirlpool or die in the attempt. Someone else just happened to remember Webb saying that he had a premonition that he would be drowned one day.

All the rest of that day, Kyle kept men posted at the whirlpool, Lewiston and Queenstown and continued to insist that Webb had made it. 'He had remarkable endurance and may have landed in some out-of-the-way place or at some fisherman's shanty along the banks,' he kept saying. There was great excitement when two bodies floated ashore at Lewiston but they turned out to be two Indians, and the day ended with Webb still not found.

At noon the following day, Kyle telegraphed to Webb's wife: 'Poor Mat has not turned up yet. I hope to find him before morning.' Her grief and fear can only be imagined. She had believed utterly in her Mat, left behind her family and friends to follow him on the exhibition trail and now it looked as if her idol had turned out to be fallible after all. In Niagara, the gossips turned their attention to Mrs Webb. She was said to be a wealthy woman, the owner of $3,000 and some valuable real estate, presented to her by her husband. McCloy had obviously talked, and Webb's small fortune was now common knowledge. Kyle tried to dismiss these stories but ended up only fuelling them. 'The stories which have been circulated about his money are false,' he said. 'He left £1,300, which is invested in England in such a way that the income is about £200 but his wife cannot touch it, as it is settled on his children who are to get it when they come of age. His wife is virtually left without anything.' Kyle was equally mistaken; at this stage, Webb's affairs were in such a confused state it is unlikely that anyone, himself included, really knew how he stood.

Uglier stories were beginning to circulate that Webb had merely joined the long line of suicides at Niagara – something which enraged Kyle. 'Anyone who holds an idea that the Captain committed suicide must be crazy,' he said. 'Why, he had everything to live for. He was a young man being but 34 years old, and he had a beautiful wife and two little children, which he thought the world of and was always talking about. He was just as well and in as good spirits the day he perished as he ever was in his life. His wife had such perfect confidence in his ability that she trusted him to accomplish whatever he undertook. Why, everybody who met him was immediately drawn to him and had the most implicit faith in him.'

Was it suicide? There is evidence for it in the will-making, but that is hardly conclusive, and in the vagueness of his plans for after the swim, but that can be as easily put down to confusion and indecisiveness. Against the suicide argument is his cheerful manner. Could he really have played the happy, confident man for weeks to his wife? But he had talked wildly to Watson, and while not actually contemplating killing himself he was probably deranged enough by then to think that he could do, and reckless enough not to care what happened to him if he didn't succeed. His lifestyle was precariously built on betting and he had become accustomed to speculating with his body. He'd known great and early fame and then slid downwards in an undignified rush towards folly and shame. Perhaps the comparisons with Hercules were not so strained. After completing his 12 labours, Hercules also ended up as a freak show, a slave to the Queen of Lydia, dressed in women's clothes, listening to storytellers singing of his former greatness. Webb was a gambler – with money, with his health, with his reputation. Niagara was simply the latest and the highest stakes.

At 10 o'clock on the evening of 25 July, Kyle called off the search, offered a reward of $100 for the recovery of Webb's body, collected Webb's belongings from the hotel and departed for Nantasket to tell Madeleine that her husband was missing, presumed dead.

Chapter 11

Oh, That is Not My Mat

He was full of hope for a prosperous and happy
future. Alas, it never came. The rapids which he
felt sure of mastering and thereby enriching
himself, destroyed him and sent him to a speedy
and pauper-like burial, and while he sleeps in
death Niagara's torrent sweeps on untrammelled,
defying the puny arm of man yet declaring the
might and majesty of Him who 'Holdeth the
waters in the hollow of His hand'.

_____ 'Lessons from the Fate of Captain Webb', a
sermon preached by the Reverend John Gordon of
Washington Street Church in Buffalo, 8 August 1883

Richard W. Turner, a mason and bricklayer, was rowing his boat
past a small cove on the Niagara River a mile and a half below
Lewiston, when he saw a man bathing. At least that's what he first
thought. But something about the swimmer must have disturbed

him, perhaps the stillness looked wrong or unnerving, because instead of rowing on he steered his boat nearer to take a closer look. Whoever it was wasn't swimming, the body was just moving with the water. Closer still, he reached out a hand, touched the man and realised he was dead. The corpse wore red silk trunks and there were cuts all over its back and bruises on the head and shoulders. On the top of the head was a ragged cut, about three inches long and so deep the skull was exposed. The body lay face down, the arms and legs extended as if the man had died in the very act of making a swimming stroke. The flesh was bloated to double the usual size, and a thick white deposit covered the skin. Understandably Turner didn't want to see the face and, without turning the body over, he hauled it to the shore, installed it in a boathouse and went to summon help. Turner knew about the disappearance of Matthew Webb four days earlier and was sure he'd found him. As soon as he alerted the people in Lewiston, a small crowd quickly made its way to the river bank where the poor bloated body lay.

'It's not Webb,' said one man decisively. 'He had a blue anchor tattooed on the right arm, and I defy anyone to find it.' Someone entered the water and lifted the right arm and roughly scraped away the white coating. There, in the swollen flesh, was stamped the blue anchor.

They left Webb's body in the care of a half-drunk sailor while arrangements were made for the post-mortem. Only then was he taken to an undertaking room. Poor Webb: his talent and good nature had been exploited for the past eight years and now, in his death, came another sort of vulture – the medical men. At least a dozen doctors who wanted to be the one to perform the autopsy rushed to Lewiston as soon as they heard the news. In the end, it was carried out by Drs Edward Smith and M. S. Long, whose report was eagerly seized on by newspapers and printed in all its gory details. The body was 'in an active state of decomposition, but no bones were broken and none of the injuries except the wound three and one half inches long in the cranium were sufficient to cause death. The cranium wound,' they decided,

was produced after death. All the blood presented a distinctly red colour, showing that it was not deoxidised by asphyxia in drowning, but that death ensued prior to that condition. None of the characteristic symptoms of drowning were present nor was there any local injury sufficient to death. It was therefore concluded that death resulted from the shock of the reactionary force of the water in the Whirlpool Rapids coming in contact with the submerged body with such force as to instantly destroy the respiratory power, and in fact all vital action, by direct pressure from the force of contact. The shock was of sufficient intensity as to paralyse the nerve centres, partially desiccate the muscular tissues, and forestall death by drowning. The conclusion was therefore reached that no living body can, or ever will, pass through the rapids alive. The river bed at the Whirlpool Rapids is much narrowed and suddenly assumes great precipitancy. The water strikes the unyielding rocky banks with great violence and by reaction meets with such resistance as to form in the centre a mountainous ridge of encroaching waters from 20 to 30 feet in height. Into this Captain Webb was submerged after passing the first breaker, and instantly subjected to the immense pressure indicated upon his body. This caused his death.

In layman's terms, Webb was crushed to death by the weight of water in Niagara.

The following day Kyle brought Madeleine Webb to Niagara. Dressed from head to toe in black, her only piece of jewellery her wedding ring, fighting back tears, she came to see what remained of her husband. Young though she was, she showed dignity and courage and refused to be sheltered from any information. Kyle took her to the river bank where she exclaimed: 'Why, there is nothing there that my Mat couldn't do.' He showed her the rapids and she promptly declared that her husband could easily have swum them and must have died when he hit the jagged rocks at the mouth of the whirlpool.

From there they went to the cemetery where Kyle tried to

persuade her not to look at the body, but she insisted. In the stultifying heat of the vault, the mortuary attendant removed the sheet. Madeleine Webb looked down and immediately cried out: 'Oh, that is not my Mat', and became so distraught that Kyle struggled to lead her out into the sunlight.

She was in deep shock, talking all the time about her children who were being looked after by Mrs Kyle at Nantasket Beach. She kept showing people their photographs. 'The boy is a perfect image of his father,' she kept saying. She was totally bewildered, barely able to comprehend what had happened; she'd been so sure that her Mat would be successful in Niagara. 'I had the utmost confidence in his doing it,' she said. 'I urged him to do it. Mat told me he could do it and he never told me anything he could not do.' He was a man of science, he'd studied the rapids carefully. She seemed desperate to have people believe that he had swum the rapids. At times she sounded as deluded as her husband. The rapids were just a mill pond compared with what he had swum. She even believed in his inventions.

It was explained to her, as tactfully as possible, that burial had to take place immediately. The corpse had already started to decompose and it was too hot to leave it unburied for much longer. She agreed and, on 30 July, the body of Captain Matthew Webb, the first man to swim the English Channel, the fêted and adored hero, was given a pauper's burial in a potter's field. Madeleine intended to return and give her husband a proper burial but, on this occasion, there was no service, no prayers, just a naked, battered body in a rough pine box being lowered into a heart-shaped plot of ground in a cemetery between Niagara Falls and the suspension bridge. Immediately afterwards, Madeleine and Kyle departed for Nantasket Beach.

Behind them, they left the doctors quarrelling. After the post-mortem, other doctors had got their wish to examine the body of the famous swimmer and disagreed loudly with the official findings. They claimed either that he had drowned or that the blow to the head had killed him. The coroner seems to have lost patience with the conflicting opinions and finally declared that he had died of unknown causes. There was confusion everywhere. His death certificate recorded drowning as the cause of death and got his age wrong, putting it down as 33. It all seemed in keeping with the mess his life had become.

News of Webb's death struck his family in England with horror. His sister-in-law, wife to his older brother Thomas, heard the news from a newspaper reporter and had to tell her husband. Thomas was overwhelmed with grief. He had no idea that Webb was even in Niagara; he was appalled by the idea of swimming Niagara but he knew that he would never have been able to stop him. No one could talk Webb out of doing something once he'd set his mind on it; he had an iron will, he said. Grief-stricken though Thomas was, he could not say that he was surprised; for some time now, he'd been afraid he would hear bad news of his brother. He spoke

Webb's death certificate, issued at Niagara, 1883.

movingly of him, calling to mind his generosity and good nature; he also had a touching faith in Webb's inventions. On 4 September, Webb's sister Mary, who lived in South Africa, drowned herself, it was reported, from grief at the news. This last story seems to have been a bit of newspaper invention, a Gothic twist to a human tragedy. She died, it is true, but in a riding accident.

Old friends rallied round, to remember his Channel swim, to deplore Niagara and to raise subscriptions again, this time for his widow and children. The Beckwiths organised a special benefit at Webb's old haunt, the Lambeth Baths. Willie Beckwith, Agnes, George Ward, Atwood, the man fish – all his old crowd were there. Professor Beckwith did a display of ornamental swimming, splendid in full evening dress and opera hat. The event was watched over by a wax model of Webb, produced for Madame Tussaud's and lent for the occasion. The real Webb would have loved to have been there.

People were struggling to make sense of his life. *Land and Water* came to praise him but ended up burying him with disapproval, lamenting: 'The sad death of a man who might have lived with credit to himself and his country. He had become an actor in sensational shows, and dependent for his livelihood upon repeated displays of a startling kind, and he felt himself compelled to go on adding to the morbid attractiveness of his attempts until at length he flinched from no hazard, however terrible.' *Bell's Life* chose to believe the stories of the railway companies' involvement and scornfully laid the blame for Webb's death at their door: 'Strangled to make a Yankee holiday and to swell the dividends of the shareholders in a Yankee railway, let that epitaph be placed upon the tombstone of Matthew Webb.'

Watson wrote: 'Remembering vividly his fate and knowing how happily he lived throughout his tempestuous roving career on the broad Atlantic, and in many lands, I have scores of times thought whether it would not have been even better for poor Webb if the mighty waves had engulfed him when he plunged from the *Russia* in his courageous attempt to effect what, despite his Channel swim, was the noblest work of his whole life.'

Disappointment and disapproval may have dogged Webb's last days and infected his obituaries. Fortunately, the future looked brighter for his memory. In swimming itself, in long-distance swimming especially, it is for ever green and fresh.

Epilogue

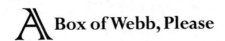 Box of Webb, Please

The Channel swim is the greatest psychological
test on this planet. You do it on your own. It
makes no difference who you are, and there's no
expensive equipment that can improve your
chances. It's a sport that has not been corrupted
or tarnished in 100 years. It's pure adventure.

_____ *Tom Hetzel, Channel swimmer, 1975*

Webb's body still lies in Oakwood Cemetery but now it has a
monument above it. His widow returned to Canada in January 1884
and ordered a granite column to be built over a new, permanent
burial site. The Freemasons paid for the simple Episcopal service
and in the snow of a Canadian winter, Webb was finally laid to rest.
On the casket Madeleine put only: 'Matthew Webb. Died July 24th,
1883. Aged 35 years.' No mention of the Channel, no mention of
Niagara. Six years later, a tree was planted over his grave. Madeleine
also opened a shop in Niagara and called it Captain Webb's Indian

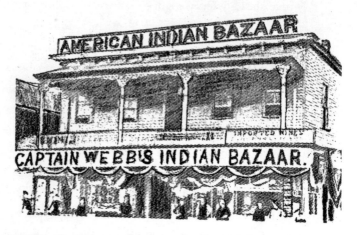

Webb's widow's attempt to cash in on his name and fame.

Bazaar; her marriage had clearly taught her something about the uses of fame. She later remarried and moved with her new husband and Webb's children to South Africa. Webb's son, Matthew, the little boy he trained to be brave, died in the First World War and Helen became a dance and swimming teacher, after overcoming her mother's reluctance to let her children into deep water.

Webb now lies between the hermit of Niagara and Annie Taylor, an elderly lady who went over the Horseshoe Falls in a barrel and survived. The oddest part of her story is that she insisted on taking her cat with her. One wonders what he would have made of such neighbours in life. Or they of him, for that matter.

Over time, the folly and waste of his last years were forgotten and only the Channel triumph remained, although not even that was untouched by controversy. It was so long (36 years) before anyone else managed a crossing that there were always doubters ready to declare that they did not believe Webb had really swum the Channel. In 1907, some of the men who accompanied him swore signed testimonies to the effect that Webb had accomplished his famous swim 'without any aid or support whatsoever'.

There are other monuments, one on the seafront in Dover and one in a depressing little shopping precinct in his home town of Dawley. The Dawley one bears the inscription: 'Nothing great is easy.' George Toms was so proud of piloting Webb across the Channel that the fact is recorded on his tombstone. There are other quirkier memorials. For 86 years Webb appeared on matchboxes, standing there in his bathing suit, hand jauntily on his hip, commemorated every time a customer asked for 'a box of Webb, please'. He's had streets named after him – there is still a Webb Crescent in Dawley – and public houses. One, opened 30 years ago, employed the world's worst copywriter to advertise itself: 'In 1875, Captain Webb set the pace by becoming the first man ever to swim the English Channel. Now, in 1969, The Captain Webb – Shropshire's *first* new Threlfalls house continues to set the modern pace – for *great* evenings out. Celebrate your next great achievement along with the rest of today's pacemakers; cut along to The Captain Webb.'

History has remembered Webb only in isolated flashes but his real and lasting monument surely lies in the spirit of all the men and women who, since his crossing, have tried to swim the Channel.

Channel swimming is about stories. Every single one of the 500 or so people who have swum the Channel has their own tale to tell. Add to that the failures, the quixotic many who try again and again, and you have almost every sort of narrative; they are brave, foolish, funny and often touching. There was William Edward Barnie, who slugged whisky throughout his training and swam into Dover wearing a sprig of heather in his rubber cap, to become the first Scotsman to swim the Channel. And Florence Chadwick, who lost 5 lb in weight during her 1950 record-breaking swim and collapsed, exhausted, on a bed of seaweed, sighing 'How comfy.' And Tom Hetzel, a New York policeman, who tore the ligaments in his shoulder during one attempt in 1969. He was about to give up when a friend shouted from the boat: 'I thought New York cops were supposed to be tough.' Hetzel changed his mind, swam for another hour and made it.

Some stories are painful, the most poignant being that of Jabez Wolffe, who made his first Channel attempt in 1906. When he died 37 years later, he'd tried 22 times and never once succeeded. On one occasion, he gave up just a few yards from the shore. And there was Ted May who applied to take part in a group Channel swim in 1954. When he was rejected he decided to go solo and started swimming from Cap Gris Nez with the inner tube from a car tyre supporting a coffee tin containing a compass, two bottles of rum, sliced chicken, sugar and biscuits. The sea washed the chicken and biscuits away and the weather turned so bad that Ted gave up after five hours and decided to swim back to France. Fortunately, he was rescued by a passing boat. But he was determined to try again. The French police warned him he would be killed out there but he replied, almost as Matthew Webb might have done: 'All the same, I'd like to try.' The police confiscated his passport but he slipped into the sea anyway. The following day his inner-tube raft was spotted floating in the Channel, and three weeks later May's body was washed ashore in Holland. Most of us would regard May as crazy but, speaking at his funeral, the Bishop of Rochester said: 'In him was the same stuff which has enabled man to stand on top of Mount Everest.'

The same stuff maybe, but not the same success; the Channel forever reminds us how fine is the line between heroism and folly.

Publishers' Acknowledgements

The publishers would like to thank the staff at the Ironbridge Gorge Museum Trust for their assistance in supplying the pictures for this book. The pictures of Paul Boyton on pages 80 and 96 come from Boyton's autobiography, and are reproduced by permission of the British Library, shelf mark 10881A39.

Every effort has been made to trace and contact the copyright holders of all photographs which appear in this book. The publishers will be glad to rectify any omissions at the earliest opportunity.